JIM MORAN:

THE COURTESY MAN

Inside the heart of one of the most successful marketers in the automobile industry

Jim Moran

Bonus Books, Inc., Chicago

05 04 03 02 01   5   4

Library of Congress Catalog Card Number: 95-80898

International Standard Book Number: 1-56625-044-7

Bonus Books, Inc.
160 East Illinois Street
Chicago, Illinois 60611

Composition by Point West Inc., Carol Stream, IL

Printed in the United States of America

To my family and the people I have worked with who have made our company the success we are.

Table of Contents

Foreword

I consider it a great honor to write a short foreword for this book because it is about one of the pioneers in U.S. auto retailing. And it's also about a long-time friend. A record of Jim Moran's accomplishments will be useful to people in this great industry—both in America and in Japan.

I first met Jim Moran in Miami in 1970, shortly after he became the Toyota distributor for the five southeastern states. I remember him as a courteous host who showed me his home and the Miami area.

I have visited Florida many times since that first meeting—often accompanied by my wife—and we have come to appreciate and greatly value our personal relationship with the Moran family. In fact, our family-to-family relationship has grown quite close over the years. I particularly remember one weekend trip to the Bahamas on the company's boat that involved a lot of fishing and swimming.

In business, Jim Moran and I have a meeting of mind and spirit. His philosophy and practices are similar to my own approach of *genchi genbutsu* (on-site hands-on). He visits dealerships often to talk with dealers and customers and to stay in close contact with the market. Like me, he always test-drives new Toyota products before anyone else in his organization and gives us his very professional feedback—both positive and negative. And we listen and react because we have great respect for his love of and knowledge about the auto business. He has always had a clear grasp of what will and what will not sell in the American market and his knowledge and advice have been of great help to Toyota. Over the years, much of his advice has been incorporated into products such as Corolla, Camry and the Lexus LS400. I particularly remember his advice about interior color co-ordination in some of our products in the 1970s.

With this short letter, I lend my voice to the chorus of congratulations to Jim Moran on his 75th birthday and to our distributor Southeast Toyota (SET) on its 25th anniversary.

Eiji Toyoda
September 1994

Over the years, Jim Moran has strived to be number one. He has always worked hard to be the best at whatever he did. Jim was a pioneer in automotive retailing and he brought that same entrepreneurial spirit to Southeast Toyota. Under his leadership, SET has grown to be one of the world's largest automobile distributorships. Toyota Motor Sales, U.S.A., is proud to congratulate Jim Moran, the associates of Southeast Toyota and their tremendously successful dealership organization on reaching these major milestones.

Shinji Sakai
President and CEO
Toyota Motor Sales, U.S.A.
September 1994

Preface

I did not want to write this book, thinking in my own mind who would care to read it, and was extremely reluctant to do so. I resisted encouragement to write it over the past five years. Some of my family and some of my very best friends— including Bob Barnett—insisted on it. Dr. Toyoda wanted me to write it and to do so with an eye toward making it a movie. While I respect him greatly, I spent more of my life interrupting movies for a commercial than doing things that would make my life an exciting Hollywood script.

As I see it, there's not much in my life that people would want to read about. There have been ups and downs and not a lot of action. I'm lucky to have spent nearly my whole life in a business I really like. Almost all people who *hate* their work fail at it. Some people *love* their work...and still do badly at it because they don't know how to maintain balance. So, what you're about to read is an account of a person who likes his work and the people whom he's met and those with whom he's had the pleasure of working.

Although I have had many "highs", there have been "lows" too. Back in 1984, I entered a plea to various tax offenses. That whole process took a lot out of me—physically and mentally—and was truly a low point in my life.

Even out of such difficulties, some good often comes. In Chapter 7, you will read about the Youth Automotive Training Center of Broward County and its wonderful accomplishments. The YATC arose out of my community service obligation in conjunction with the plea agreement. Ironically, out of one of the low points in my life came one of the accomplishments that I am most proud of.

I really wanted to wait to write this book until I was free to comment on some other matters as well. Being a large and diverse company, we have had our share of litigation. I could write a book about that and I hope to do that someday. It will be very interesting and revealing.

What finally swayed me to write this book was feeling the obligation to write *our* book and not *my* book—a chronicle of the great people with whom I've had a chance to work over the years, especially those at JM Family Enterprises and Southeast Toyota. It's my deep hope that "our book" will document some of the most memorable contributions which our people have made to the evolution of the American automobile industry—and those contributions by the people I work with have been many.

Acknowledgements

The list of people who directly and importantly contributed to this project is a long one. First, there's Harvey Rumsfield, who is still on the job at 81 today and who helped reconstruct the anecdotes and the history of the early years. Then, there's Hal Barkun—for years my loyal and ingenious advertising counselor—who really enabled me to bring our early days on television to life. Herb Tousley, who just passed away a few months ago, was one of the brightest, most intelligent people I ever met. One word describes Herb—integrity. Marilyn Boesken—my loyal and highly effective Assistant for more than two decades—helped greatly in organizing my thoughts about the Florida years. Bob France, Ed Dalton, and George Herbert—who made such important contributions to creating our systems and facilities in Florida—helped me to recreate that era.

Dick Knox, who built Jim Moran & Associates, was responsible for the evolution of our warranty company—making it one of the largest in the world—and for the development of our insurance company as well. He also hammered out the foundations of World Omni Finance and helped put the YATC school together. Since he has touched so many aspects of JM Family, you can imagine the importance of his role in this story.

The late Charlie Melchiorre was the person who really freed up Dick Knox so that Dick could initiate so many innovations on behalf of JM Family. Charlie was the kind of a guy who could keep the relationship between the parts and service departments running in an effective, low-key way. In a big operation, that's not usually an easy thing to do.

My son Jim did a first-rate job of developing our marketing program and especially our television campaign as a Toyota distributor. My son-in-law John McNally came up from the lowest ranks in the company to the presidency on his own merits. Our future owes a lot to his guidance and insight. His wife—my daughter Kitch—has been exceptionally supportive of John over the years and has been a good mother and homemaker, very much like her own mother. Jim, John, and Kitch have contributed a great deal as members of our board of directors since the very beginning. You'll hear a great deal more about our current president, Ms. Energy Plus, my daughter, Pat Moran, who will be heading JM Family Enterprises in the future.

As I said, Bob Barnett pushed me over the wall to try being an author and persistently kept after me to move the writing along. Bob also contributed to the editorial guidance for the book. In addition to Bob, I cannot express my gratitude enough to our other attorneys at Williams & Connolly for their wise counsel on this project and so many others throughout the years. Hats off to Ray Bergan, Doug Marvin, Dan Katz and so many others on that wonderful team.

Inside our organization, Wayne McClain was the guiding light and "point man" whose judgment and urgency helped make this book possible and steered this book along its development. As always, Larry Rich offered superb insights and counsel. Information on the technical side of things came from what I consider to be the finest group of management administrators in the automotive retailing business anywhere. That group includes such people as Bob Arnett, Colin Brown, Ken Czubay, Casey Gunnell, Darryl Head, Ed Machek, Dave Majcher, Michael Nixon, Logan Pierson, Dave Reduzzi, and John Williams. John Whalen was very helpful in writing the section on the Youth Automotive Training Center.

We couldn't talk to every one of our dealers, but we have the greatest dealer body in the world—I love them all, and there's not one whom I could fairly single out. My "Little Brother" at Toyota Motor Sales—the recently retired President Yukiyasu Togo—offered some great perspective, as did the current TMS President Shinji Sakai. Jim Press, Senior Vice President and General Manager of Toyota Motor Sales USA's Lexus Division, gave his usual astute insights and once again proved how much of a special friend he is to SET and to me personally. Jim Olson did a superb job of coordinating communications for us both in California and in Japan. Of course, that Honorary Chairman E. Toyoda would honor this book with a personal introduction means a great deal to me.

Dr. David Fry, the President of Northwood University, gave his usual provocative and intelligent assessment of the direction of the automobile industry. I'm indebted to Rabbi Merle E. Singer and his wife Myra for their knowledgeable guidance on community action programs and enlightened philanthropy. One-time Little League star and currently Chicago commercial real-estate dealmaker Alan Chapman helped me reminisce about my days coaching Little League.

Gail Stanley is not only a model for what an Assistant should be in every respect—she also did a fabulous job of coordinating the endless logistics and details that went into the writing of this book and did so in her typically good-natured way. Administrative Associates such as Marge Stafford and Sandy Pipkins also helped keep the ball rolling. Chet Hall did a first-rate job setting up the systems for editing the text.

My collaborator, Ron Beyma, has my deep and sincere thanks. He is a true professional—and a great guy on top of that. He is astute, sincere, and diligent. This book could not and would not have been written without him.

Finally, there are members of my own family. Although she didn't know if writing this book was a good idea at the outset, you couldn't imagine a more dedicated supporter than my wife Jan. But she's like that in everything on which we collaborate in our business and personal lives. I also have to thank the rest of my family for their patience and confidence during the lengthy and time-consuming process of writing this book. That includes my three children, their spouses, seven grandchildren, and three great-grandchildren—the first had her third birthday in February, the second was born in August 1994 and the third was born in June 1995. Another is on the way.

Some notes about how this book is organized: Interrupting each of the seven chapters is a management message of about two pages in length. I call these little essays "Tell It Like It Is"—which is the same title that we have used for years on similar communications to people in our dealer network. In fact, a couple of these commentaries are actually adapted from essays that first made the circuit inside Southeast Toyota. These discussions are not necessarily the bible, but they sum up important lessons for me and may be helpful to others. I've tried to set these thoughts apart so that they don't slow down the business autobiography which is the main part of the text.

Finally, there are three other concessions that I have made to my editors. Frankly, I'm not comfortable with any. From time to time, you will run across quotes from other people in the book. Often, they're about me. Since we're a private company and we haven't had nearly the coverage that many other businesses our size have had, the editors were adamant that those quotes stay in to help give people a clearer picture about JM Family Enterprises. The second concession is the one "Tell It Like It Is" *not* authored by me, but by Rabbi Merle E. Singer—the piece in Chapter 7 that discusses our community involvements. I only relented when the editors insisted that the community story is such a central part of the firm's story and that of its people. So be it. The third is the Afterword, authored by Dr. Melvin Stith, Dean of the Florida State University College of Business. His comments are kinder and more gracious than I surely deserve. I hope that's the way in which people will read these sections because that is certainly the spirit in which they are being offered to the reader.

Jim Moran
Deerfield Beach, Florida
November 1995

Working with Jim Moran

When this assignment was first offered to me, I was immediately drawn by the chance to get inside the head of one of the great living talents in modern marketing. In no sense was I disappointed.

When you meet Jim Moran, the first thing you notice are those piercing blue eyes. Bright, penetrating, intelligent. You know at once that he's sizing you up, and you can sense that he's doing a pretty good job of it. The second impression is the disarming, low-key sincerity of the Moran manner. He makes you feel genuinely comfortable...at ease and on an even footing.

Jim is a polite, forthright person. You never find him to be short on candor, nor is he—for a minute—overbearing. Unlike many people of his stature and fame, one doesn't ever sense that he's posturing or playing a role. It's been an absolute pleasure to work with the people of JM Family Enterprises, and these folks sing Jim Moran's praises from the first to the last soul I met. I spoke with a number of Associates, but I never came away feeling that any of the comments were contrived. Clearly Jim has touched many of his colleagues on a very personal level with his concern, his generosity, and his leadership.

Any writer knows that the best authors are natural storytellers, but they must also have enough of a teaching instinct to link each story to a lesson. Thinking and talking in this style are second nature to Jim Moran. His "Random Access Memory" for events, details, and settings that are often half a century old is amazing. Since I'm a marketing consultant as well as a writer, the sheer rightness and plain-talking sensibility of his marketing principles intrigued me. Jim is a marketing thinker of great clarity.

Finally, the most powerful impression with which Jim Moran leaves you is his appreciation and concern for people. People on all levels. People in all kinds of roles. A sense for people evident in many ways. From gracious hospitality...to a sympathetic ear for a small problem. An admirable self-discipline is—I think—the backbone of this respect for people. You see it in those few gifted souls who have made great achievements from modest beginnings and who are determined to think about their own humanity and that of others in the same honest, basic way today as when they started out.

Ron Beyma
September 1995

1

A Wagon Ride to the Gallant Lady

1918–1939

Perched on the flying bridge of the *Gallant Lady*—a 167-foot Feadship motor yacht—I gaze at the shore as our captain gracefully slides the ship into the harbor off Abaco in the Bahamas. On the shoreline ahead, I can see a little boy yanking his rusty red wagon loaded with a case of empty soda-pop bottles. He's a handsome young man, perhaps seven or eight...and native to the Islands, I'm sure. Clink-clink-clink. I can faintly hear the bottles rattling against each other as the youngster yanks the wagon's rusty black handle, making his way along the dock. The sights and sounds of the shoreline take me back to a very different time and place.

Instead of the pristine sands of the Bahamian Cays, my mind's eye recalls sand of another sort. It's the sand, gravel, and clumps of crabgrass along the ragged first-base line of a baseball diamond in the Near North Side of Chicago. The year is 1925, and it's the Dog Days of August. The sun is as baking and relentless as in the tropics...though there is no ocean breeze to ease it. But the sound I remember is the same—bottles clinking together. In this case, full bottles sliding down into my mother's wash tub as the throbbing sun melts the ice surrounding them into a slush.

One week earlier I turned seven. Vermont-born Calvin Coolidge is president of the United States. And I'm at my favorite place in the whole world—one of the four baseball diamonds by Senn High School. It's a Sunday afternoon, and there are four ball games going on. My love of baseball drew me to Senn every weekend. I'd watch and watch, but, after that long summer wound on, something started to tug at me as much as the baseball action did. It was really basic, and it affected all the people around me—the guys on the field and the girlfriends and onlookers down the sidelines. People looked it, acted it, and even said it. Everybody there was *thirsty*, and there wasn't a drinking fountain in sight.

So I decided to do something about it, and that's what made this Sunday special. The way I figured it, this was my chance. That August weekend in 1925 was my debut as a vendor...a grassroots service industry...a retailer. My first day I sold two cases of pop from my mother's washtub propped up on a red wagon. When people knew they could get something to drink, business just kept getting better. For a piece of the action, one of my older, bigger friends carried the crates of twenty-four eight-ounce pop bottles from our storage cubicle in the basement over to the ballfield. On my biggest day, almost six cases or nearly one hundred and fifty bottles were sold. The only real limit on my sales was the hundred pounds of ice I would buy from the ice factory on Winnemac Road—ice that friends also helped me haul to the park. Even before the last bottle had gone, those big hunks would have melted away and that meant I was out of the refreshment business for that day.

The tub was jammed with frosty bottles of root beer and "rainbow flavors" such as cherry, orange, raspberry, strawberry—all Hire's. No Coke. Coke cost a cent a bottle more—three and a half cents versus two and a half. Since I sold pop for a nickel a bottle, selling Coke would have driven quite a dent into my profits. Because they were thirsty, people would drink whatever they could buy, and Hire's was a quality beverage. To me being the "pop boy" was a vein of pure gold, and I mined it for two straight years.

Me and my wagon...From the very start, I guess, my fortune was tied to four-wheel vehicles. And, the funniest part of all is—while I have always loved cars—my greatest pleasure has really been boating. Maybe one enabled the other.

Today, life looks a little different from the bridge of the *Gallant Lady* than the cobblestone and concrete world of Near North Side Chicago. This three-story yacht is one of three owned by JM Family Enterprises. Twenty-three hundred Associates and their families rely on JM Family Enterprises for their livelihood, and the thirteen separate businesses that make up this company form a diverse mix. The biggest of our subsidiaries is Southeast Toyota, the largest franchised Toyota distributorship in the world—serving the five Southeastern States of Florida, Georgia, Alabama, and the Carolinas. Last year, we sold over two hundred thousand cars, trucks and vans through our dealers.

Our other businesses are substantial, too. We own the biggest Lexus dealership in the United States, massive distribution parts and processing facilities that support our distributor network, a sizable computer company called ITS (Information Technology Services) that handles the information needs in all of our firms, World Omni—a considerable finance and leasing company, and JM&A Group —a full service insurance and warranty sales and marketing firm. We've had the good fortune to enjoy dramatic growth. If you compare 1980 with 1994, our revenues of fourteen years ago were a little over nine hundred million dollars. In 1994, total revenues were nearly *three and a half billion*.

Did it all begin with squeezing pennies out of pop bottles? It began, and it thrived, because of people sharing in a dream and working hard to achieve it.

Now may we back up a minute? You could be asking: Just where did Jim Moran come from, before we find him tugging a wagon across the baseball diamonds of Senn High School?

Well, my mother's name was Anna and my father's was James. They were first-generation Americans. My father came from County Mayo in Ireland, and I know very little about his family. He had a brother who died in a drowning accident before I had the chance to meet him. I never met my father's parents. My mother—from whom I inherited both my white-blond hair and my blue eyes—was an only child. She hailed from Stuttgart (an auto capital in its own right) and came over when she was very young as her parents sought to avoid the Kaiser's army and the endless wars. My mother's parents died when I was a toddler, and I have little recollection of them except that my mother's father was an iron worker who made fences and worked with steel. People I called Uncle or Aunt as a kid were really just family acquaintances.

My parents had five children; but only I and my sister, Genevieve, who was born seven and a half years earlier than me, survived past childhood. She had M.S. since she was 42. She passed away not long ago and had a difficult time in life, but her religious faith held her in good stead. Some of the warmest memories of my early childhood were attending Mass with Genevieve around the Christmas and Easter holidays at St. Gertrude's, our parish church. As with many poorer Catholic parishes of the time, the church was in the basement below the school. *Education first* was the principle. I can still remember the candles flickering against the bricks during mass in that basement, the simple pine-branch decorations around the altar, and the beautiful above-ground church that was later erected—going up limestone by limestone.

My dad ran a United Cigar Store. People say that he was friendly and outgoing, and that I'm like him in that respect. Maybe so. In those days, you would find a United Cigar Store almost on every corner of the big cities like New

York or Chicago. In some ways, they were like the convenience stores of today. They sold cigars, cigarettes, pipes, tobacco, newspapers, candy, gum, and magazines. The store even served as a laundry drop-off and pick-up point—an important plus for the customers who lived in nearby rooming houses. My dad worked from 1 PM to 1 AM, so we never saw him much. That kind of job tied you down seven days a week for $12.50 in wages and no benefits. There were plenty of others ready to take over if you didn't like the terms.

We lived in a cold-water, walk-up flat on the fourth floor of 1543 Granville on the North Side of Chicago. The rent was $27.50 a month including free decorating—I wouldn't call the wallpaper patterns designer quality, though—and electricity, a storage room in the basement and one month's concession (or free rent). I can still remember the dingy gray oilcloth that covered the kitchen table. It was so drafty in winter that you thought the hallway was a wind tunnel. If it sounds like this was rock bottom, it wasn't. When my father died, we moved into an even more modest place.

I went to a parochial elementary school—St. Gertrude's —run by the Order of the Blessed Virgin Mary. Tuition was $1.75 a term, and you would always present it to the nuns in an envelope rather than handing them cash directly—if you had it.

The neighborhood had a real mix to it with Irish, Germans, Italians, and plenty of other nationalities. You could find members of every big religious denomination in the area. Because you never knew what you'd run into, you didn't go out of your neighborhood much; but sometimes we were curious and adventuresome, as kids are bound to be. Five or six blocks away there were nice homes in an area called Rogers Park that sold for $5,000 to $7,000. I'd see kids from "over there" in the neighborhood or in school, and they would be dressed a little bit differently. They weren't wearing fraying corduroy knickers or worn and tattered shoes. Not only did they dress better, but they got allowances and real presents at Christmas or Chanukah and on their birth-days. I saw that there was a different kind of life literally just around the corner, and money seemed to be the heart of that difference. When your family doesn't have much, you're looking for ways to make money to help out. That's what drove me in my early years.

I always wanted to be successful or to amount to some-thing. In the early days, I never was. Neither a very big nor strong kid, I still loved sports with a passion—although I was an average, not a great, athlete. But there was a burning desire in me to show others that I could do something, even though I had nothing. To this day, I still feel a need to make a contribution, to have an impact on things every morning I get up. It's fading a little as I grow older, but most of the old *chutzpah* is still there.

From wagons, I graduated to cars; and they have been the central theme of my life to this very day. After my soda pop business, I started to wash cars in a three-car garage in back of the apartment where we lived on Granville. People on the block would rent space for their cars in the garage. They would leave early in the morning and not return until six or seven at night. I got to know them and took care of their cars. They let me use the space to wash other people's cars; and, on Saturdays, some would even pull their cars out so that I could use the space for my car wash business. The price was 25 cents for a wash and that included vacuuming out the seats and floor and "detailing out" (carefully clean-ing) the instrument panel and the steering wheel and then scrubbing the white-wall tires and wire wheels.

When you're young and trying to work to earn money this way, it's often tough to develop close friendships. One exception was a pal named Eddie Mulvihill, who was one year older. We used to wash cars together. Later, when I had my first gas station, he came on the payroll—but not right away because the business couldn't afford it.

Car washing gave me my first chance to run a car. I say "run" because it really wasn't driving. Fifty feet forward and back in the alley is as far as I would risk taking an auto, but it was enough to teach me how to shift. I was careful, fearful that the owners might resent someone fooling around with their cars. Really learning how to handle cars came later at the gas station, moving them off the lift or to the side of the property.

Persistence in finding paying work was a trait of mine at a very early age. I can still remember my mother—who spoke both English and German—shaking her finger at me and saying with an exasperated smile: *"Ach, du dickköpfiger Weißkopf!"* which means "Oh, you stubborn towhead!" But it probably helped to pay the rent.

> *"Mr. Moran has achieved extraordinary success and prestige through his lifetime of hard work and dedication to the automotive industry. Even with his busy schedule, he devotes much of his time and energy to those less fortunate, particularly children, displaying a genuine interest in their well being. This is a man who has never forgotten his roots."*
>
> — *Logan Pierson*
> *Group Vice President,*
> *JM Family*

There wasn't enough business behind our home to satisfy me. The next step was to visit various gas stations in the neighborhood and to solicit Simonize jobs. I'd bring my own pail, chamois, sponges, and wheel brushes and wash the cars right by the station. If I was lucky enough to get a wax job too, I'd move the car to a shady spot. For the wash, I'd still charge a quarter; and the station would get 50 or 75 cents from the customer. To Simonize, I'd collect $3.50 from the service station, and they would charge the customer $5 to $10. While at the station, I picked up some on-the-job training on how to change batteries, grease cars, and fix flats.

Simonizing meant $1.25 out of my own pocket— 75 cents for the can of wax and another 50 cents for the paste that you used with it. So my costs worked out to about forty-two cents a car and plenty of elbow grease. The only other investment was for baby diapers to do the polishing, and my mother would wash them out at home for me.

Until the age of twelve, work meant odd jobs on cars or anything else I could find. A friend of my mother owned a meat market over on Morse Avenue in Rogers Park. The owner hired me, and I would deliver meat orders all over the neighborhood. Never a single tip—not a dime, a nickel, or even a piece of candy was given. We were in the midst of the Depression.

> *"Jim Moran is the embodiment of the American Dream. He runs where others walk. He has FITB—fire in the belly—and it's a contagious quality. Starting from scratch in Chicago, he later built a multi-billion-dollar business in Florida. His success has enabled others to succeed and, in the true spirit of America, he has always given back as much as he has received."*
>
> *— J. P. Bolduc*
> *Former President and*
> *Chief Executive Officer*
> *W. R. Grace & Co.*

No matter what I did, cars were always on my mind. While I was growing up, the car had "grown up" too from being a novelty, to becoming a mass-produced symbol of achievement (with the Model T), to being the biggest pleasure-and-status purchase a person could make short of a house. It's fair to say that we kids in the neighborhood were all car crazy. Especially during a summer evening when the apartment windows were open, you could hear cars start while you were falling asleep. Some of my friends bragged that they could tell the make of the car without seeing it just by the sound of the starter. Harvey Rumsfield, who is about five years older than me and was later on the staff of both Courtesy Motors and Southeast Toyota, says that he could guess what kind of car was coming toward him at night by the look of the headlights. Kids of my generation were steeped in product information from an early age.

As a youngster, I could spot detail differences between cars. Even though cars are very refined today, I can still get in one and tell if it is a well-balanced unit where everything works in harmony. As just a youngster, I could listen to the exhaust and tell if the engine was timed right, or if it was idling too fast or if it was loping, or if the points weren't set right or the plugs were bad. As a kid, my dream career was to be working on automobiles and getting a job in a gas station. Maybe some day—I thought—I would be able to save enough money to have my own station. But the problem of the moment was finding work.

Herb and Walter Abrams were other buddies of mine. Their dad Leo was assistant advertising manager for the *Sun-Times* newspaper in Chicago. I used to wash his car and do other odd jobs for him; and, one day, back in Depression times, he said "Jimmy, I'm going to get you a summer job as a copy boy." He did. That was the first time I met the famous columnist Irv Kupcinet. Irv didn't start as a copy boy. He had begun his career in the mail room a few years earlier. Journalism never really interested me, but I can remember running errands all over the Loop, picking up and delivering copy and ad formats, so I got an inkling of how newspaper advertising worked.

My father died when I was fourteen. At the traditional Irish wake, my mother served a ham, some ginger ale and beer. Then people passed the hat. Did I hate that feeling of dependency. In everybody's life there are milestones, moments that forever change the way that you think and live. One of mine happened in November 1932—not long after my father's death. I was on my way to school. My mother had convinced Father Dorger to let me attend Loyola High School without tuition. I could clean, sweep, and wait on tables. On that November day, the wind was brutal while walking the two-and-a-half miles to school. My jacket was flimsy and I was chilled to the bone. Why wouldn't anyone stop and give me a lift? Why wouldn't anyone have some feelings for me? It was then that I truly realized that everyone lived in their own little world. A kid on the way to school was just another kid. There were no options. I had to make it on my own.

"My Dad worked. That's the way he was brought up. It created the legacy upon which our Associates are building today."

— Pat Moran
President, JM Family

At the age of fifteen, I worked at Art Heron and Bill Murphy's Shell gas station at Rosemont and Devon Streets for a quarter an hour, and I kept the job through my Loyola High School days. Even then I loved to drive a car and still do; I oohed and ahhed over the sound of the motor and the hum of the gears. As a kid, I was really drawn to Buicks. To me, they were the best of the General Motors line. The 1938 and '39 Buicks had a peppy Dynaflash-8 engine and a chassis and drive-train with coil springs and good suspension and better handling than anything that Chrysler or Ford had to offer. A Buick was an upscale car—but only people with a solid middle-class income could afford a new one. In those days, anybody making between $30 and $50 a week was an executive. You could buy a brand new Ford for $494. A Buick Super or Special *loaded* with equipment like a radio and a heater was much less than a thousand dollars. A Cadillac was under $2,000.

Looking at cars was—for me—like window-shopping through dreamland. When I was about sixteen, I remember sizing up a Ford dealership, gawking. My nose was pressed up against the glass as though it were the world's biggest candy store. The salesman invited me in and said to me: "Son, this is our top-of-the-line Ford. We call it our 'Baby Lincoln.'" Funny way to put it, I thought, but his flair for describing a car stuck with me. As you'll see later, putting that mental image to work made me a considerable amount of money.

The learning of my earlier years was more through

watching how the world worked and through things picked up on the jobs I did than in the classroom. Education can be such a powerful tool, but it wasn't for me as I was growing up, sad to say. My high-school education didn't prepare me much for later life. Religion was taught twice a day at the Jesuit high school I attended. Strange as it may sound, Latin was the one subject with a true practical payoff. I'm convinced that my Latin studies really were the building blocks for my public speaking ability.

During ninth and tenth grades, I played sports. After that, I couldn't both play sports and work. To work the gas-station night shift meant reporting to the station by five o'-clock. I couldn't continue basketball or baseball practice and be at the station to handle my shift. Throughout high school, I worked at the Shell station. But it wasn't steady enough work after I left high school—just four or five hours a night. I needed more to help out at home.

Work was tough to find. The Depression was bitter, with twelve million people unemployed. At any major intersection, you would see World War I veterans sitting on fruit crates selling apples out of boxes for a nickel apiece. The soup-kitchen lines looked endless. The most unfortunate begged on street corners. Because people couldn't afford them, many apartments went vacant. Whole families would move into a single room at a rooming house, and an entire floor would have one common bathroom out in the hall.

"You always know where you stand with Jim Moran. Above all, he respects the people who are his Associates. Whatever business concern may be on your mind, you can always face each day knowing Jim Moran will be there for you."

— Bob Arnett
Group Vice President,
Parts & Service
SET

For any job offered, fifty to sixty people would apply

for it—even a ticket taker in a movie house. Those without steady jobs would sell Eureka vacuums and magazines door-to-door, and so—a little later—would I. When the seasonal or sale peaks hit, I sold shoes at Goldblatt's and Marshall Field's, the big department stores. Part of my plight was the Depression, part of it was just the challenge of entering the full-time job market. Young people could relate to what the actor Spencer Tracy went through when he had just started out: "There were times when my pants were so thin," he once said, "I could sit on a dime and know if it was heads or tails."[a]

> *"There is probably no better example of the American work ethic and what it can achieve than Jim Moran. He started from humble roots, but never in his life has he failed to achieve something that he set out to do. And he has always done it with a deep sense that he owes something back to his friends and to his community."*
>
> *— Bob Barnett*
> *Williams & Connolly*

In the early thirties in Chicago, most people were living from hand to mouth. I can't say that I ever went hungry myself. My German mother was a very frugal homemaker and that helped keep our pantry stocked. Since my father had been accustomed to eating Irish, that became the practice in our home. My mother kept watch over a great big cast-iron pot with a heavy iron handle to it. That pot simmered on the stove all the time. Chicken bones, neck bones, pork, biscuits, bread, soupy gravy, vegetables, and rice would go into it. *Mulligan Stew* of course. Who could forget its taste!

Times were tough, but prices—especially for food—would seem like a fairy tale today. Hermann Wolff—a German baker—concocted the greatest pumpernickel bread a person could dream of. Two huge loaves of his day-old bread cost just a nickel! Hamburger was 10 cents a pound. Stewing chickens were just 12 cents a pound. Steak? Nobody knew what it was! But the greatest delicacy was a double-dip ice-cream cone. That trip to heaven set you back just a nickel. A chocolate soda or fudge sundae cost a dime. I smoked back then: two packs of Lucky Strike, Philip Morris, or Camels—take your pick—for a quarter. At Goldblatt's Department Store, you could buy a package of off-price Wing cigarettes or a cigarette two feet long and cut it up yourself. That make-it-yourself pack would come out to about eight cents.

The economy was bad...the climate maybe worse. Chicago's winters were often bitterly cold, and there was no air conditioning to blast out the roasting, steamy summer heat. The ice man would come up and down the alley behind the houses and apartment buildings and look for the sign in the window—a sign which read 25, 50, 75, or 100: the number of pounds of ice that the lady of the house wanted to buy to chill the ice chests that were the forerunners of today's refrigerators. Coal and ice operations were often combined into a single business because people needed the coal in the winter to heat their homes and the ice most of all in the summer to keep their food.

You worked hard. You counted your pennies. You survived.

The Depression taught me that you can rebound and earn a living if you're willing to work, no matter how tough things may seem. A job is an act of trust on the part of the person who is taking the job as well as the person who is granting it. I still believe that today.

TELL IT LIKE IT IS

"People: How to Select Them...
How to Motivate Them"

People are the heart and soul of any business that I've ever run. So, selecting and motivating people is just about the most important thing a manager can do. You'll never really understand what makes a person tick unless they trust you, unless they feel at ease with you. People say that I have a knack for putting them at ease very soon when I first meet them. If true, it's a lucky gift.

I try to evaluate people looking for several key things. This probably comes from my years in selling. Three things rank first: Do they have integrity? Will they be loyal? And, will they dedicate themselves to doing a great job? Be ready to make some mistakes in your picks. It isn't all instinct, and no manager chooses people with 100% accuracy. I know my ability to pick people has become better over time.

All of my life has been spent selling. The people whom I know best are salespeople, and I've learned that money and incentives drive salespeople to perform. If you're smart and run a sales-driven business, you'll start out with the best people— especially in key spots like the sales manager. Even if you feel you can't afford them, take the risk. Odds are that the rewards will boggle your imagination. And, make sure that the attitude of finding the best people trickles down the line in sales, service— *everywhere.*

Back yourself up with a strong incentive plan and monitor it closely to make sure that the plan isn't misused or abused. Early on, the philosophy of spending a dollar to make the business five or ten more made a lot of sense to me. The people around you have to believe that they have a stake in satisfying the customer and making the business profitable. Incentive plans make it happen, and make sure that you stay with the incentives you promise. Pay plans are absolutely, positively the soul of a selling business. The best salespeople tend to follow the hot products; and the marketplace is getting tougher and tougher with new products popping up all the time. Incentives and profit-sharing are the best way to keep good achievers.

People have to know and believe they are in business for themselves as well as for their firm. "Whatever I'm doing is *my* part of the business. It's my baby," should be the way all Associates feel about their work. A manager's job is to leave his or her folks alone and to let them do what they've been asked to do. The four most important words managers can say to their people are: "*Go get it done!*"

Everybody depends on the boss. Not to make the decisions, but to keep Associates fired up. A boss either enthuses or defuses, stimulates a workplace or stops it. So, a manager's job is to build people up every day. I've never ruled by fear. There's nothing to be gained by threatening people with losing their jobs. It's always better to coach people that there must be a better way.

People are what they think they are. If you think you're great today—as a friend of mine put it—and you thought that you were awful yesterday... you're ten times better off than you were. A boss's job is to help people believe that they're the best they can possibly be. A sharp boss can boost the results of a workplace ten-fold...maybe more!

I've never tried to "manage" people. The light touch and the nudge are always better, I think, than manipulating people down to an eyelash. Things don't always go right. Sometimes people get confused. Managers who don't take time to answer intelligent questions cut their own throats. Once in a while, people don't get things done fast enough. When that happens, a boss has to be persistent for the good of the company and everyone else in it. It's not hard to be persistent but in a nice way.

People will make mistakes. Some of our best people have made big errors and come back to be better afterwards. The best thing a manager can do after somebody drops the ball is to say, "You did your best. Don't take it hard. Do something else for us." The big thing is to buoy up the person and their attitude.

Another part of a boss's job is to help people grow, even if they leave you. A number of our best people started out at the bottom. Today they're district sales managers or dealers. One of our dealers put it this way, "I will be proud when one of my own people goes off and gets their own store. It's a philosophy I learned at Jim Moran's lunchtable."

Finding what I considered to be a "real job" during the Depression meant trekking down to the U.S. Employment Office looking for a job with more money and some advancement—either in the automobile line or not. My high school diploma didn't guarantee work, but it certainly made it easier to find work than if I had no diploma at all. After a year of short stints...six days at a printing company or two days at a silk-screen processor...or maybe two days unloading a box car, I followed up on an ad in the paper for a "scull-dredger" at Graham Paper Company on 440 South Canal and got the job. It paid $12 for six days' work a week.

The job description was simple: menial work in big doses. The only expenses were lunch and carfare, which was seven cents for the streetcar each way. Back then Chicago had great big red streetcars with flatiron wheels. We lived on the car line on Clark Street and you could hear the streetcars rumble by night and day. After a while, you just tuned them out. I never rode the elevated trains much because they were a dime a ride—much more than the streetcar. The difference between a roundtrip ride on the elevated versus a roundtrip on the streetcar was more than the price of a double-dip ice-cream cone.

I unloaded trucks and boxcars, rolling around a pushcart and bringing down reams of paper from the upper floors in the warehouse to load orders into trucks. Graham was not a manufacturer but a middleman. They sourced their paper out of Wisconsin and had salesmen who would sell their lines, which included butcher stock and craft, writing, enamelled and other coated papers. I was about seventeen, and at least I was learning what a middleman did.

Although I was promoted to office boy (and earned another dollar a week) where I did filing, cleaning up, and errand running, I didn't like the job. My heart was still in cars. In a small community paper that came to the house free, a blind ad appeared one day with a box-number return address for a steady job as a service-station attendant. It was seven days a week but the weekly salary was $14. I wrote a letter and received an invitation to visit the gas station. It was a leased-out Standard Oil station on Ashland and Rogers in Rogers Park—essentially a well-to-do Jewish community. Standard Oil owned the property and the lessee was obliged to buy Standard Oil products—greases, motor oils, batteries, etc.—exclusively, like franchisees in some fast-food chains must now.

Not long after starting my new job, I remember visiting Standard Oil headquarters in Chicago—just to see what the place was like. What stuck out in my memory was a fellow doing nothing but polishing the brass in that magnificent lobby. The Rockefeller fortunes which built that company could easily have paid for the brass to be chrome plated. But, I think that Standard wanted to send a signal to all those dealers in their little gas stations, dealers that might come by to visit and admire the headquarters on an afternoon off. Every morning, at a Standard Station, you had to take out the brass cleaner and polish the pump nozzles.

Dave Guthmann, the proprietor of the Standard station where I worked, was very sharp at tuning an engine, putting in points, setting a carburetor, and adjusting brakes. I learned those things from him and how to reline brakes too. It was a vocational education for me, on-the-job training. From the moment I met him, I knew that Dave could help me learn. I worked for him at that station until I was nineteen.

"Jim Moran is blessed with common-sense brightness. Growing up humbly, he learned to read people very well and very quickly."

— John McNally
Director, JM Family

It was about then that I bought my first car—a used '32 PB Plymouth convertible with a price tag of $95. New, it cost almost five hundred dollars. On sunny days, that two-seater with its Isinglass side curtains and red-leather upholstery was a knockout. But, on rainy days, it lost its glamour quickly. The "one-man roof" generally took one man and four boys to get up and the car would turn into a bathtub on wheels before the roof was back in place. With my own car now and with the work at the station, of course, cars had become almost the sole focus of my life.

Back in my neighborhood, Sinclair was just building a new station at Clark Street and Glen Lake in Chicago. It was a beautiful building with a white terra-cotta front, two islands, two lifts, a grease rack, a wash rack, and a huge driveway. Sinclair didn't have a tenant in mind that was as good as Dave Guthmann in my opinion.

I suggested to Dave that this might be an opportunity and encouraged him to see if he could get the franchise. He didn't like doing business with Standard Oil. They were too "hands on". Dave called up Sinclair's district bulk plant. A month later Sinclair awarded him the lease. He then sold his existing lease for the Standard Oil station. Not only was the new station great looking; it was only five or six blocks from the apartment building where I lived.

The Sinclair lease fixed the rent at a cent a gallon—and the tenant also had to pay for heating coal, water and electricity. Sinclair paid the taxes. If you sold 10,000 gallons, the rent was a hundred dollars; and on 20,000 it was two hundred. With those terms, any tenant would be a captive of the supplier, and there wasn't much incentive to add volume.

I didn't know it then but that gas station, with its green-and-white "HC"[1] pumps, was to become the backdrop for an entirely different business. Mostly by coincidence, the large concrete apron on the station's corner was to launch my real career for the rest of my life.

---

[1] By the way, the "HC" stood for High Compression.

2

8 for a Buck

1939–1944

The world economy was in a mess in the early 1930s, and life took some ugly twists as the decade wore on. In Germany, the Nazi plague took root, but there were even "brownshirt" rallies in arenas and assembly halls in America. Fortunately that kind of thinking never seriously took hold here. Two high-profile athletic events pounded home the idiocy of racist thinking to common people more than a ton of preaching could have done: Jesse Owens's stunning achievement of four gold medals at the Berlin Olympics in 1936...and Joe Louis's knockout of Max Schmeling in June of 1938 in the heavyweight title fight. As a sports enthusiast, I know that these two events really said something to me. Here's what America truly meant—the opportunity for people of every origin to live together and to excel.

When that madman Hitler invaded Poland in the fall of 1939, we all knew that war was coming. Dave Guthmann was deeply patriotic, and I could tell that he would be going into the service for that reason alone. He also had a personal motivation to enlist early. Dave was Jewish and he was understandably appalled by what was happening in Europe.

One day in 1939, Dave told me that he had made a decision to sell out. "Do you want to buy me out?" was his
question. I said that I certainly would but that I didn't have
a lot of money. We went down the list of assets that he
owned: the fuel in the tanks, the tools, the greasing equipment, the tire and brake machines, the motor oil, and the
parts and accessory inventory. It all added up to about five
hundred dollars. My spirits sank. I told him that I just could-
n't do it. Then he came up with a good idea. "What if I let
my tanks run down?" he asked. He had a 5,000-gallon tank
for Pennant (the economy line) and 10,000-gallon tanks for
both regular and premium.

He let them run down so that the total station price
would be three-hundred-sixty dollars. I didn't quite have that
much and I told him so, but I *did* have $330. "Well," he said,
"the price is $360. After a month, when you've made some
money, you can send me the thirty bucks." My check to him
arrived on time. When the lease was mine, I found out that
I had to have money for insurance and other things. It was an
immediate education in managing a small business—learning
things the hard way. Outside of the few fixtures, what I had
bought was really the right to continue the lease with Sinclair. When the business opened under my name, I had
about five dollars in the till for making change. If a customer
had come in waving more than a $5 bill, I couldn't have
changed it.

*"Jimmy, the most important thing in life is to honor your
word to others. Your word must be your bond!"*

— *Anna Moran*
Jim Moran's Mother

Still I was an independent businessman with my own
gas station, and my confidence was boundless. I was determined to make my Sinclair station the number-one attraction in the neighborhood. "It's gonna be big," I told my
mother. "I'm going to work harder and better than anyone

else. It's *going* to work. Please don't worry." She stayed skeptical: "Your father worked for 35 years at a United Cigar Store. He made 12 dollars a week at a steady job. Here you are putting a fortune in this deal." And, for our circumstances, it really was one.

I nearly killed myself for the next several years to overcome her doubts *and* those that I harbored myself from time to time. You have to have determination. I opened up at 6:30 in the morning and closed at 10 o'clock at night, 7 days a week, 365 days a year, including Christmas. I had to be there sick or not.

By now, I had been around gas stations off-and-on for nearly a decade and understood how thin the margins were for peddling gas. Still I couldn't grasp why a station manager didn't build the highest possible volume. The way the rent was figured seemed to build a brick wall against your opportunity, but couldn't that be changed?

After about six months I talked with Vince Walsh, who was the Sinclair field rep and headed up the bulk plant (he later worked with me at Courtesy Motors), and said, "Look, I want to be a volume gasoline merchandiser, but I can't do it on a cent-a-gallon rent. Why don't you let me pay a flat rental and let me go for volume!" What finally persuaded him was a little hint in a question I threw at him: "How would you like to have the highest volume Sinclair station in Chicago?"

A flat rental of $75 a month with nothing escalated on a per gallon basis: That was what I wanted in return. My guarantee was simple and absolute: After 30 days, I will be pumping a minimum of 30,000 gallons a month. He said that he wanted to run my rent idea by the people Downtown, and—to help that along—came my assurance that I would buy everything from him, saying, "*I need a flat rental rate if I go for volume.* But the rent you're offering me prevents me from making money, if I pay more rent when I sell more."

The next day he called back and proposed a half a cent a gallon. He asked, "Why are you so stuck on $75?" Because this station can sell *more* than 30,000 gallons, was my answer. Well, he said, if you'll give me your word and guarantee me that you'll sell 30,000 gallons of gas in 30 days, I'll put this new lease through. In reality, I sold over 40,000 the second month. They gave me the new lease for $75...and they tacked on a new minimum for oil sales.

When I look back at that negotiation, it was one of several points in my life when I stepped forward and took a risk. My decision wasn't backed up with any fancier analysis than some numbers penciled on the back of butcher-shop paper. I just figured that if I could do things a little differently and couple hard work with building as much volume as possible, things would work out.

> *"People ask me to describe the essence of Jim Moran. Do you have a week? When I meet with him, I feel reinvigorated with the true values of life. He has made so many people successful. Not only a great marketer, he truly understands people, and their motivation."*
>
> — *Sid Wolk*
> *President, The Cross Country Group*

For the first year and a half at the station, I had no help. On Saturdays and Sundays, I would hire a couple of kids to help wash cars and to service the pump. Only a little later did I bring in help that was more experienced. For now, the inside would be my job and the young fellows would take care of the outside. But I was always worried if I'd stay healthy. "Will I be able to open the station tomorrow?" would be the question on my mind whenever I felt a cold or flu coming on.

My lease gave me a real pricing advantage, including being a cent per gallon lower than most other stations. I cut the price of the gas, but attracted more oil, battery, and tire sales; brake jobs; and lubrication and wash business in doing so. *I learned how to create opportunity out of the steady supply of customers that I had.* From opening time until 9 AM, we could hardly do anything but pump gas. Afterwards it would be wash and lube jobs all day.

"Jim Moran likes to shoot straight up. He has a gift: He can visualize what can happen with the right people."

> *— Hugh Woods*
> *Retired Executive Vice President,*
> *World Omni*

The Shell dealer across Clark Street tried to meet me on price, but he found out that he couldn't make any money. Daredevil customers would cross the car traffic buzzing down Clark Street just because we were one cent a gallon less. Customers even told me: "The minute that you're not a cent a gallon less, we're going right across the street." Hunting down penny differences in gasoline pricing is still a game for people even to this day. Choosing off-brand fuel and self-service all add up to those pennies today. It was true then, and it's as true now: *Small price differences remain the heart of competition in volume merchandising.*

When I was alone during the week, I washed enough cars to fill up Wrigley Field, or at least so it seemed. The toughest part may have been the cold-water washing of the cars. In frigid temperatures, my hands would be soaked in freezing cold water, and I would run out and pump gas. Right afterwards, I'd hustle back and go on washing. The pumps didn't have the valve controls that they do today. They would back up on you; the cold metal of the pump, the cold water on my hands along with the kerosene I would use to clean the grease off, and the gasoline itself would all collide to make one stinging experience. I still have scars from the infections that festered on my hands and eventually wound up wearing rubber gloves at the station to protect my hands.

But there were bright spots. In 1941, I married Arline Steveley, a lady who was both a wonderful wife and an outstanding mother. My father-in-law had a drugstore on the corner of Granville and Clark Streets. He'd see me as he was walking to open his store at 7:00 AM, and I'd still be there when he closed up at 10:00 PM. Even though my in-laws were concerned if I would make it, my father-in-law would often say, "I've never seen anybody work as hard as Jim." My mother-in-law was also very supportive. She would tell my wife: "Arline, you don't know how lucky you are. Some day," my mother-in-law would say to her, "it will all have been worth it." And I believe that Arline herself felt that came to be true even though a severe chronic ill-ness...and an even more devastating "cure"...were to mar her later years. She spent the last years of her life in a wheel chair.

The confidence that Arline's parents had in me meant a lot. In my mind, I had the rough idea of a business plan, al-though I'm embarrassed to call it that, because it seemed so crude and simple. HARD WORK and COMPETITIVE PRICING were the first two legs on which I built my business. The cheapest gas was 8-for-a-buck...7-for-a-dollar-fifteen on the regular. On a sale, you made half a cent a gallon, and if you weren't there, customers would just drive on through to the next station. In those days, if someone bought two dollars worth of gas, you had to practically overhaul the car: Check the tires. Remove the seat to top up the battery, because that's where batteries were then. Unbolt the battery box. Fill the battery. A customer watching you would say: "Gee, there's a little corrosion on the terminals. Would you mind getting a wire brush and cleaning that up and add a little grease?" Then I'd check the water in the radiator. But they'd always say, "Don't bother with the oil because I've got oil at home in the garage." Bought during bulk promotions from Sears, Roebuck for a dime a quart, no doubt. Some cus-tomers would even expect the same service for just a fifty cent gas purchase.

A lube job—and I mean a total job—ran 50 cents. For the high fliers who would buy oil at the gas station, oil was 16 to 36 cents a quart. Repairing a tire with a hot patch was 35 cents. That included installation and rotating the patched tire to the spare mount and the spare to where the damaged tire had been. I could do a little bit of mechanical work like brakes and clutches. But that was good when you could get it.

At first, I bought my tires from a Pontiac dealer about half a block away. In those days, dealers would take off tires—black-wall tires that were actually called "take-offs"— and replace them with the increasingly popular whitewalls. These "take-offs" were in great supply and they were nearly new. After a mile or a mile-and-a-half, some still had the rubber pressing cleats sticking up through the grooves.

You could buy them for $4 a piece and scrub them, and sometimes I even touched them up with a black gloss so they looked as new as they were, but I always explained to customers that they were take-offs…and that this next-to-new merchandise could save $4-5 a tire. Not long afterwards, I was selling 75-100 tires a month. When the Pontiac dealer figured out what I was doing, my source of supply dried up. The dealership started selling take-off tires itself for less than I was charging. The Firestone store two blocks away gave me a way around that. Wally Mager (who passed away about two years ago) ran the store, and *his* pile of take-offs was even bigger than the Pontiac dealer's. I made a deal with Firestone to do basically the same thing I had done with Pontiac.

Hard work and pricing were two legs that underpinned my business, as I said earlier. But, a third was needed: AD-VERTISING AND PROMOTION. Eventually, I had the largest volume gas station in the city of Chicago. That took about three months to accomplish. In gasoline, Sinclair back then stood on the bottom of the brand ladder compared with such prestige brands as Standard or Shell. But this experience with an also-ran brand taught me an attitude that proved to be invaluable during my days selling Hudson cars.

The station's former owner, Dave Guthmann, was a great guy who wanted to make a nice quiet profit, but he didn't want to promote—no price signs or wash signs. (By the way, after I had later become a local success on television, Dave was still concerned about my success and wanted to help me out. He used to send me nieces, nephews, and other customers to buy cars. Dave and I were always good friends.) But I had to change the station's image through more advertising. That meant stringing up a huge sign over the parkway between the sidewalk and the curb, which was a 10-foot stretch. I put up another sign, 20 feet high and 8 feet wide. On the top it read: "Jim Moran", figuring that people liked to entrust the care of their car to a *person* and not just some brand name...and to set my station apart from all the other dealerships. Below my name was the price of the gas: 7 gallons of regular at $1.05, 7 gallons of high-test at $1.15, 8 gallons of Pennant at one dollar.

> *"I know this guy and have great respect for his integrity and his ability to deliver something that is unavailable anywhere else, whether it be a piece of product, service, or kindness. Jim Moran has played a pivotal role as automobile marketing has changed more fundamentally than at any time in its history."*
>
> *— Dr. David Fry*
> *President,*
> *Northwood University*

Another sign went up over a gravel area where cars were parked. This was about 15 feet long and 8 feet high with the slogan, "A Perfect Car Wash: 75 cents". These were all lettered and detailed by a professional sign maker. Since nobody else was doing this sort of thing, some competitors jeered at the commotion I was making, but others started doing the same thing.

Even price, hard work, and simple advertising weren't enough after a time. Dealers started to compete through promotions, which are just another kind of advertising, and we were no exception. We even started some of the premium give-aways in Chicago.

Half a dozen glasses with ten gallons of gas.

A pitcher, sugar bowl and creamer with ten gallons and an oil change.

When you sat down to figure out where you'd make your money some months, it was enough to drive you dizzy. It got the job done, but a dealer still had to give all the service, despite the promotions. After it was clear that we were leading the market, competitors really laid into us. The other dealers who just preferred loafing to real competition had the worst attitude. They would come in and say, "You gotta take that sign down. You can't sell gas like this. You're ruining the market." My message to them was: "You run your business...I'll run mine. It's a free world, and that means free competition."[2]

---

[2] Most people think that those big fabric signs whipping in the wind over a gas station are tacky. I chuckled recently when I browsed through Thomas Hoving's memoirs. Hoving was the most distinguished and revolutionary Director of New York's world-renowned Metropolitan Museum of Art in current memory. One of his first innovations when he took over was to mount a huge banner over the building's fancy facade promoting the Museum's blockbuster shows. The Museum still does it today, and hundreds of other museums now do it too. Hoving knew what I knew: Big signs sell.[b]

TELL IT LIKE IT IS

"The Best Sell is the Straight Sell"

Salespeople often ask me: do you believe in the hard sell or the soft sell? I really believe in the STRAIGHT SELL done in a soft way. *Tell it like it is.* And, in a courteous, knowledgeable, and believable way.

It doesn't make any difference if it's insurance, washing machines, or cars. Selling anything is essentially the same. You have to project yourself positively and honestly.

Make a friend out of the customer. A qualified salesperson probes for and listens to the customer's needs and desires. If you want to make a sale, get at the buyer's motivations quickly, or you won't be able to focus their desires on the right product. It may sound funny, but the role of the salesperson is to kindle the romance between customer and car.

How does this all work in practice? Not long ago, some of my colleagues asked me: "How would you go about selling the '95 Corolla?" Figuring that one good example is worth more than dull theory...and since the principles don't change...here's the approach I suggested:

Greet the customer at the door, thank him or her for coming into the dealership, and establish whether he or she is interested in the Corolla. Tell the customer that you would like to explain this completely new automobile.

I'd start by thanking Toyota for building the finest quality cars in engineering, styling, performance, longevity, and resale value. First, it's true, and second this impresses the customer you have such respect for the manufacturer.

Then give the customer a complete walk-around, stressing the all-new round, flowing styling ("Looks like a baby Lexus, doesn't it?") It is no longer a sub-compact, but a compact. "It's almost as roomy as the first Camry." Then point out that the Corolla is one of the safest cars built—with dual-side airbag, supplemental restraint systems, and optional anti-lock braking. Then I would list all the features it has as standard equipment not available on competitive makes: The larger engine—bigger than the Honda Civic and Nissan Sentra. Among these three, Corolla has the most torque at low RPM's, the widest-tread tires and biggest wheels, and a firmer, more solid ride. It has the most leg room, the most shoulder room in the front, and the most hip room front and rear.

I'd tell the prospect about the 4-speed ECT automatic transmission available on the Deluxe and LE models. Corolla offers the best warranties: 3 years, 36,000 miles overall with 5 years, 60,000 miles on the power train. Rust and corrosion are covered 5 years with unlimited mileage. In short, the Corolla is a much bigger and radically all-new car.

Let the prospect know that they haven't experienced anything until they drive the car and then take out the keys to the demo. For this car, the test drive is the real closer. The Corolla positively sells itself. The handling, acceleration, stable-but-soft ride, complete tightness of the body, and extreme quietness at any speed are astonishing. To top it all, the car has superior cornering, turning radius, and firmness. It is a car anyone will enjoy driving—quiet, peppy, smooth riding, and extremely economical.

For the demonstration drive, I had a definite stretch of about five miles picked out. It included a railroad-track crossing, the roughest road possible, and, above all, some room to get the car up to at least 55 MPH. Keep the radio off, so the prospect can experience how quiet it is and hear the soft rumble as it goes over railroad tracks or washboard roads. A thorough demo ride will turn a skeptical customer into an anxious buyer.

This kind of sales presentation can't be done in less than 30 minutes, but—if done right—it works. Because of the fine product and the approach. When the sale is closed, the selling isn't over. While the car is being prepped for delivery, the salesperson introduces the customer to the service manager who will take care of that car. So, the customer has a personalized contact point for car care. "Sales sells the first time. Service sells the second time." The very next day after the purchase, the customer gets a call from the salesperson or the manager asking the customer if they were satisfied. Nothing builds customer goodwill and confidence more than that call. The truth is we're not selling a car. We're selling a relationship.

Two years before leaving the gas station to enter the Army, I had two helpers who could do simple mechanical work, and that's when I first started using incentives to boost business. In addition to their flat wages, I paid these young men a nickel on a quart of oil, 25 cents on a lube job, 15 cents on a tire change. At the end of the day, we filled out a tally sheet. It might amount to as much as three to eight dollars. If a helper rang up $50 in commissions in any given month, he got an extra $10.

All the incentives tied product knowledge to extra effort. They were simple. And they worked too. The staff actually had a personal reason to look under the hoods, to check the fan belts, and to ask customers about oil and filter changes, tire rotations, and shock absorber checks. Would they normally ask these questions? Of course not. No normal person would, because it meant extra work. They would have to do it and not get paid for it. I wanted each of my guys to be the *first ready service person to perform any needed work*. A dime or a quarter got them to solicit the business. My philosophy was simple: Tie in the wages of my Associates to a percentage of the company's profits. Give them a reason to work for the percentage "more".

The service incentives were one part of a bigger service picture. That included a friendly greeting to every arriving customer and politely asking how we could help them. A principle learned in my earlier days from Dave Guthmann at his Standard Oil station also made a difference. Standard Oil took it so seriously, I can't help but think that it was the Golden Rule of a Standard Oil station: *Greet the customer at the pump!* Be there and tip your hat as they drive up. Tell them about specials. Ask them if they need oil. SERVICE then became the fourth element in my business approach. I think it was also the one that made the biggest difference.

Beginning in 1941, the whole mood of the business, my customers, and the neighborhood changed as our country entered World War II. People banded together more as they saw war on the horizon...but they were nervous, too, as loved ones left for Service. Despite the War, things started to improve economically even before the U.S. entered the fray. Everybody was employed—either in Service warming up for a foxhole or bending metal at a factory.

> *"Working with Jim Moran is like being in the backfield with Gale Sayers. It looks easy, but it's so hard to duplicate."*
>
> — Al Hendrickson
> Owner & General Manager,
> Al Hendrickson Toyota

The bombing of Pearl Harbor and the tragic sinking of the *Arizona* first reached my ears as I was doing a brake job. That bulletin heard over the gas station's old Emerson radio hit home on many levels, and I knew that my life would soon be changing. I continued to run the Sinclair station until I went into the Armed Services in the summer of 1942. Although leaving my business and my young family made me glum, I was anxious to do my part. The station was left in the hands of my brother-in-law. I didn't stay in the service for the entire tour of duty. The Army insisted on releasing me due to a heart problem. (That coronary problem—a defective aortic valve—was to catch up with me later in life when I underwent a triple bypass operation and the replacement of that valve.)

After my medical discharge, Arline met me in California and we drove back to Chicago with my eldest daughter—who was just a baby then. (Her official name is Arline, too, but we called her "Kitch" because of the way that she scooted around the kitchen floor in diapers.) We didn't get much sleep on the long trip back, but before going home I made a beeline for the gas station. It was during a typical Chicago winter, and the fresh snowfall amounted to six to eight inches on the ground. I don't need to tell you that the first thing that you do in the wintertime in a gas station is to clean the driveway. Otherwise, the islands are covered with snow, and the customers get their feet wet if they step out of their cars. Also, you can't do any service work by the islands because you're not able to put a jack under the car when the snow builds up.

Turning the corner off of Clark Street, my heart sank: My beautiful gas station had turned into a sleepy little ice palace, with just two tire tracks leading up to the pump. My brother-in-law sat in the office toasting himself on the radiator. It turned out that he couldn't wash cars or change tires because he had rheumatism and had hurt his back trying to put a car on the lift. All he could do was gas cars. The business had withered away. It was going to be like starting all over again.

That setback was one of the most upsetting moments in my life. The station's decline had been going on the entire time I was in the service. There were no more regular customers. When I asked my wife why she didn't write or telegram me about what was happening, she said, "What good would it have done?" and she was right. It would only have gnawed at me, over the thousands of miles.

"For all his wealth and success, he's still so down to earth. His generosity is low-key but significant, just the way he is. There are not many people around like that anymore."

> — Don Bowen
> President and CEO
> Urban League of Broward County

Since nearly everyone was in the Service, and you couldn't get help, Sinclair was glad even to have my brother-in-law there. Gas was rationed. The OPA (Office of Price Administration, a department of the federal government created during the War) would issue consumers a coupon book. For 30 coupons a month, you could get $4 of gas. The prices of gas, food, and automobiles were frozen during the world hostilities and for very good reasons. But, while the War had people competing for their very lives on the front lines, an era of regulations, quotas, and shortages began back home. Those conditions were to last into the 1950s.

On my return in 1943, the reconstruction job I had to do on the gas station business was tough. To bring the customers back, I sent a personal letter (no photocopies in those days) to all my regulars asking them to try us again and telling them that I was back, that their business would be appreciated. If anything had happened while I was away, I wanted them to understand that it was none of my doing.

Although the shortages were just a fact of civilian life, I'd be lying if I didn't say that they also worked to my initial advantage. I didn't intend it that way. They just did. By the time 1943 rolled around, there were just no cars to buy. General Motors was welding together Sherman tanks. Chrysler was assembling cannons and Army trucks. The auto plants were all engaged in defense work. No cars were built between 1942 and 1945-46. *That meant used cars suddenly acquired an entirely new value.*

"Jim Moran never says I would like you to work for me. He always says I would like us to work together."

> — *Ted Pass*
> *Retired Vice President,*
> *Fleet Sales*
> *SET*

In 1944 I dipped my toe into the used car business. The first car that I sold on the gas station apron was a 1936 Ford Coupé. It was bought from a customer who lived down the block for $75. One day, he came in for some gas and told me he'd be going into Service soon and he had to sell his car. He said he hated to do it. I asked what he wanted and he said one hundred dollars. I offered him seventy-five dollars *cash*. The cash offer cinched it. He said he would just as soon sell it to me as anybody else.

That's the way it started. At the time, I didn't know what the car would actually be worth—only that, if fixed up, it would be worth more than my purchase price. I installed a new distributor and clutch, relined the brakes, steam-cleaned the motor, and hand-waxed it to a sheen. Parts and supplies may have cost me all of $35.

When sold, it went for $275—just $20 less than the $295 price sign that I placed on the windshield. The price on the sign was just a wild dream of the most that I thought the car might bring. A hundred sixty-five in profit! Where had I been?

Right away, I tried the same thing again, this time with a Packard. The net was even better. So I started selling cars one by one and paid attention to how each customer *bought* the car. Other stations started doing the same thing I was doing. What made me different from most station owners who displayed cars was my telling a prospective buyer exactly what was done to improve the car and what *wasn't*. I would say: "If the car isn't right, bring it back and I'll fix it for you." Almost always, I would get nearly the asked price because I knew the car, its prior owner, and its real condition.

In selling anything, you must earn the customer's confidence to the extent that you make a friend out of them. Before they buy, *they* know what *you* know.

> "To put it simply, Jim Moran knows how to catch the heart of the deal. He's not only a salesman but quite a philosopher, too. In contact with our Japanese managers in Nagoya, he catches the vibrations of Japanese psychology and people's minds and adjusts himself to them."
>
> — Yukiyasu Togo
> Retired Chairman,
> Toyota Motor Sales, USA

Even though I had achieved a lifelong ambition in buying a gas station with just a few hundred dollars in savings, I could feel that car sales were the inklings of a new business. From that day forward, my ambition was to get out of the gas station.

3

The Coming of
Courtesy

1945–1955

After a string of successful car sales waged from the gas station, I gave the original Sinclair station to my brother-in-law and started branching out. At first, I didn't consciously settle on the business of being a car dealer exclusively. Ultimately, I owned three gas stations and then added a garage near Loyola University. Owning three stations—by the way—was a business strategy that didn't work at all well: another lesson for me. You can make as much money when you have one gas station as when you have three. You can't be everywhere all the time. Some of those grease jobs, tire changes, and mechanical labor charges ended up lining the pockets of others. The way to get beyond running a single gas station, I quickly learned, was *not* to become a proprietor of a string of gas stations.

It was time to follow my nose, and my nose told me to get into the car business. By this time, I had $5,000 in my own capital and borrowed another five from the bank. I used it to start up my own used-car business on a rented lot on Broadway having enough space for ten or twelve cars. The lot was right across from a Walgreen's drugstore and a 200-foot long cosmetics factory. It was the home of Maybelline, and the founder would park her glossy red Auburn speedster, with its motor-boat back, prominently beside the factory entrance. Did I envy her taste in cars!

Not long after I opened the "United Auto Mart", it soon became one of the largest used-car operations in the city. What made my niche in the marketplace? Simple. Nobody was taking the time to clean the cars up, detail them, do the body work, and even do the simplest mechanical work. Our cars looked and performed better than our competition's.

As far as my life was concerned, car retailing was a different world from any I had ever known. Instead of low-wage manual labor or being chained to a gas station and on duty or on call three quarters of the day, I was either hunting for cars or waiting for customers to come in. I kept a Rolodex file with a card on each of the cars I owned. The data included what I paid for it and the costs of parts and labor to recondition it. The salesman drew 10 percent of the profit. At this point, the lot had two salesmen, a mechanic, and a car polisher/clean-up man. I would primarily do buying and help sell on the weekend. It was easy to control the business because I had set a rock-bottom selling price on each car for the salespeople.

My target was to make $300 per car after commission, and generally we did. I thought I had died and gone to heaven. My brain was in action a lot more and my hands a lot less. I certainly wasn't using them to wash cars in freezing water and running out to the pumps soaking wet when the next car rolled over the bell cord. Was it really possible to make money this easily?

The key to the used-car business was buying right, which allowed you to "turn them over" (sell them) fast. I seemed to have a knack for that. Success with the space on Broadway led to a little bigger operation on Ridge and Clark Streets where I rented another lot and then started my own motor clinic. Having garage space again enabled me to apply what I had learned at the gas station, which once more enabled me to seriously rejuvenate and refurbish the cars before placing them for sale. The property itself was leased since I couldn't afford to buy real estate.

At Ridge and Clark, my maximum inventory investment was $20,000, and the cars on hand—in which that money would be invested—would vary from ten to twenty units. The object was to sell those cars as fast as possible. Cash flow was always a problem. So, I looked for reasonably priced cars that I could turn over quickly rather than big, expensive Cadillacs or Lincolns. I targeted the mass-market customer who could spend $500 or $1,000 on a popular, reliable used car.

As enough used cars became tougher and tougher to buy, I widened my scope. Surprisingly, dealers themselves were one of my best resources. Ford and Chevy dealers were making so much money because of the pent-up demand for new cars that they didn't want to be bothered with used cars. Many dealers at the time considered it beneath their dignity to sell used cars. They also didn't know the product as well as they should have and were afraid of making costly mistakes in buying used cars.[3]

One retailer who shunned used-car sales was a Ford dealership on Halsted Street in Chicago Heights way south of the city—in fact farther south than Hammond, Indiana. About every two weeks, I'd stop in there and buy a used car or a used truck from them. I'll call the man who owned the lease "Fred Fiveiron". He was never there. He had been a "tel-e-grapher" for Ford Motor Company and had made a

---

[3] It was the old chicken-and-egg problem: The reason dealers didn't know the various industry products well enough was because they weren't in the used-car business. If you *were* in it, you had the chance to study and to learn the strengths and weaknesses of the other makes. But they never decided to pay the price and to learn. Being constantly stung by making mistakes buying used cars made them reluctant to be in the used-car business. So, they just sat on the sidelines.

friend out of the zone manager who gave him this small dealership. The location wasn't worth much, but it got its allocation of a few cars a month, which suited "Mr. Fiveiron" just fine because he liked to play golf. In a time when cars were scarce, dealerships were just a cozy little franchise to mint money.

One day in 1945, I finally ran into "Mr. Fiveiron" himself; and he asked *me* if I intended to be in the new car business some day. I told him that of course I would like to, but that dealerships were so scarce that owning one would be too rich for my pocketbook. He asked me if I'd like to buy *his* dealership. I told him that I would *like* to but that I didn't think that I could afford it. He seemed anxious to sell.

"It only gets four or five new cars and three trucks a month," "Fiveiron" said. "If you were to buy me out, you'd probably have used cars, and maybe you could make some more money on the back-end of the business." One word led to another and we struck a deal for $20,000—most of that money having been earned in my used-car transactions.

It's a paradox: Everybody associates the *used*-car industry with sleazy tactics. In my experience, the first time that I had to come up against truly sleazy tactics was when I first started selling *new* cars. Because new cars were still so scarce when the War ended and immediately afterwards, many dealers expected (and many customers were willing to pay) money under the table to get a new car. The dollars changing hands were large. A dealer would often charge from five to fifteen hundred dollars in cash for the chance to buy a new car.

Of course, some dealers tried to find ways to make the maneuver look respectable: Instead, for example, of taking a car in trade that was clearly worth $1,300, they would only allow $300 toward the purchase price of a new car and simply pick up a thousand dollars worth of value for nothing. In the business, that gambit is called *trading a customer out for nothing*. I wanted to do away with practices like that and to establish myself as an honest retailer. The customers loved me for it, but was I ever in for a rude awakening a little later…from a very unexpected source!

I was making a mistake by not going to Ford directly to buy the dealership. But how could that be avoided? If I went to Ford Motor, they would have another "Fred Fiveiron", another "tel-*e*-grapher", another friend to whom they would give the dealership. So, I bought the stock in the dealership from "Fiveiron" and ran it as "Fred Fiveiron" Ford, which was perfectly legal. No under-the-table payments. I did everything by the book—I sold every new allocated vehicle for the OPA list price.

Business boomed. Our little dealership was stretched to the hilt. The Chicago Heights Ford location was no Taj Mahal. Behind the one-car showroom, there were three service stalls. We didn't have a used-car lot. The staff I inherited included a salesman, a service manager, a bookkeeper, and three mechanics. In months, we had a thriving used-car business, too—despite the space problems—and were of course quickly selling everything that Ford shipped us.

At first, I expected new car retailing to be a little more glamorous than life at the gas station or on the used lot; but I also quickly learned some lessons about people buying a car in a new car showroom. One of those lessons was to never look down at a potential customer. Someone sporting boots and bib overalls, or tube tops and tattered sneakers today, can be as intelligent *and* as financially able a car customer as anybody wearing a suit with a tie or a designer scarf. I well remember the first customer who came into my dealership in Chicago Heights. He was a hog farmer who wore thigh-length boots hitched up by suspenders, stained with manure, and plastered with straw. Had I been a salesman, I might have taken a pass. Instead I walked up and greeted him. He turned out to be a displaced farmer from the Old Country. In a few minutes, he bought a new car and paid cash with a wad of bills that popped out when he yanked off his left boot. He was the first of thousands of customers to give us their trust as we steadily built a reputation for fair dealing. But the smooth sailing was about to end. I should have expected it: After a while, a number of other local Ford dealers were up in arms. What was I doing by selling cars at the official list price?

One day a factory rep came out and said: "I never hear from 'Fred Fiveiron' any more." He doesn't come in very often, I explained. "I can also see that you're selling a lot of used cars," he went on, "and, another thing: We don't get any complaints about customers coming in and you wanting a thousand dollars under the table." He wanted to know if business was being done differently, and I said maybe. In any case, we were selling cars strictly off list price, I emphasized. He looked bewildered. When he left, something inside me said that I would be seeing him again.

One Saturday several weeks later, the same guy dropped back "on his own time" (or so he said) and wanted to buy me lunch. Over the lunchtable, he said that he was sure that this wasn't "Fred Fiveiron's" operation any more...but, that's life, he chuckled. "We appreciate that you have done a good job for us and that you tried to get us some repeat customers for Ford. So, we're going to let you sell out," he said...as though he were doing me a favor. STUNNED was the only way that you could describe the look on my face.

They weren't going to hurt me, he pledged, but "they" were sure that I had bought "Fred Fiveiron" out. "What do you mean that *they* won't 'hurt me'?" I asked suspiciously. He explained that somebody else who was a friend of the zone manager wanted this franchise badly enough to agree to build a brand new $40,000 facility. The new owner was going to relocate the dealership on the main boulevard. "Everyone" wanted to avoid lengthy negotiations and legal hassles. *They* would give me six months time to get out and would allot me five extra cars a month and four extra trucks a month to make me feel better. The factory suggested that I "find something else to do." The verdict was final: "We don't want to be tough; but, if you don't do this, we'll cancel you." They wanted me out of the system. I wasn't bitter at Ford, but I *was* disappointed in the manner they acted.

Ford didn't like me because I made them look bad, bucking the herd as I was. An attorney friend of mine told me that I better do as they said. The Ford rep had ended his speech by telling me point-blank: "We may be making the biggest mistake we ever made, but you know how it is." It was the age-old Code of the "Good Ole Boys" Club: "Your buddies deserve a shot at the easy life." I bit my lip and gave him a little homespun prophecy when our lunch-time conversation ended: "Some day, it's going to change. You're going to need someone at your dealerships who will work hard." In a way, it was fine because I certainly had no intention of building a $40,000 palace for Ford at the time. My first fling with Ford had come to an end.

It was January of 1946, and Ford was soon going to make me a dealer without a franchise. About a block away, the window of a vacant car showroom was waxed over. The sign above it still said Hudson. Maybe here was an alternative. At least I was curious to learn more.

"In the face of his own personal adversity, Jim Moran has an uncanny knack both for coming back and for making others around him feel good about themselves."

— Dr. Joseph Kump

In 1946 Hudson Motors was just treading water. Their car looked like an antique taxi cab. The hood opened at the windshield instead of the front bumper. Worst of all, the Hudson had no GO...and no true styling. The car was sturdily engineered but ugly. The firm had essentially been building the same car for ten years, and it was mechanically perfect. But what a styling catastrophe! From the shark-nosed front end to the sorriest excuse for a dashboard that I had ever seen.

With that vacant dealership on my mind, I went down to Hudson's beautiful regional offices at 1234 South Michigan Avenue at 8:30 the next morning. The son of Hudson's Chairman Roy Chapin ran that office. I told the receptionist at the switchboard my name and my interest, and she told me in a friendly way that I was wasting my time. Hudson wasn't adding any dealerships or opening any territories and didn't intend to do either. She said that Hudson could sell twice the number of cars that they were building. I persisted and asked if I could talk to the manager about the vacant dealership in Chicago Heights. He wasn't in yet, but she said that I could wait.

After a while, a tall, good-looking, well-dressed man came in, and I was ushered into his office. He repeated the receptionist's message telling me that Hudson wasn't expanding its dealership network and that he didn't want to waste my time, but he appreciated my interest. He didn't even remember the closed dealership a few miles beyond the city limits. I wouldn't give up. "How about the future?" I pressed him. "How about two or three years from now when the demand for cars slacks off?" I told him that for every car he gave me today, I would sell two later when times are tough. His position didn't budge. He wasn't convinced that I could do what I promised, so I thanked him and left politely.

The next morning I was back again asking for five more minutes of his time. He said that I didn't know when to give up. These drop-ins went on for a week. The turning point came two days later. When a store becomes available in Chicago, I told the young Mr. Chapin, *I have an ad campaign that could sell a hundred Hudsons a month*. He stared at me with sheer disbelief: "Nobody sells a hundred Hudsons a month," he said, "either you're crazy or I'm getting soft. Let me think about it." The next day he said that he couldn't create a contract in which he could commit me to guarantee two sales later for one allocation today, but that I impressed him and that he would call his father. He wanted his dad's thumbprint on any decision, but his father was on a fishing trip in Canada. After a phone call, Chairman Chapin sent the decision back to his son and the dealership was mine. My return visits to Michigan Avenue worked. I've achieved more through "polite persistence" in my life than through any other style, and this was a case of it.

Thirty days later we had the Hudson franchise, and I had the great pleasure of canceling my Ford relationship *early*. I stopped selling Fords *before* the six months expired. They ended up with no representation in that trading area because the new Ford dealership facility wasn't built yet. When I called up the Ford zone manager to break the news, he was flabbergasted. He wanted to know how many cars I was going to get. When I told him thirty cars a month and all the trucks that I wanted, he couldn't believe it. I sold the Ford parts at a discount for $8-10,000 to another Ford dealer. The Ford logos came down, and up went a freshly painted sign that read "Midtown Motors"; and I was in business as a Hudson dealer in the spring of 1946 in the same location where I had been since 1945.

In the fall of '47, Hudson introduced its 1948 model. The Car of Tomorrow they called it, and it looked like one. Their advertising slogan captured it: "Here today...the car of tomorrow." It featured the sensational "Step-Down" design look which was elegantly ahead of its time. It was called "Step-Down" because it was low-profile and hugged the ground. There was a four-and-a-half inch well that you had to step over, hence the term "Step-Down". All the other manufacturers ridiculed it, but today "step-down" styling is the state of the industry. The Hudson came in three versions: Pacemaker, Super 6, and Commodore 8. In 1950, Hudson came out with the Hornet. The "Step-Down" look kept Hudson in the design spotlight until 1953. Hudson also made a two-passenger convertible called the Hudson Hollywood with a big 6-cylinder engine in it. A pretty car!

As we got to know the new Hudson more intimately, we learned what was under its skin-deep beauty. The new model was stunningly designed—wide and low slung—and it was fast enough to chalk up plenty of wins on the stock-car circuit; but now the durability and the quality of construction of the car were frankly disastrous. The new frame and welding processes had to be debugged. When it rained, water would trickle down from the roof onto the driver's knees. On a sandy road, dust would swirl through the passenger cabin because it wasn't sealed properly. The manufacturer never really focused on these problems enough to find the cause of the leaks. All a dealer could do was to try to putty over the leaks under the dashboard, and we did the best that we could to tackle these and other mechanical and construction problems that the car had.

Because new cars were still so scarce (every Hudson to be built up to the year 1950 was on a buyer waiting list), we never advertised new Hudsons in the paper. The newspaper ads were strictly for used cars. You would think that with a new-car waiting list customers could at least expect to get the car that they had ordered. Not on your life. The factory would build what they wanted, and this continued even into the fifties. If a dealer sent in orders for 10 Super Six Sedans or Club Coupés, and the factory had the metal and the parts to build Commodore Eights, that's what they would make. More profit could be made on the more powerful cars—all loaded with Drivemaster transmissions, wheel covers, whitewall tires, directional signals (which were still optional then), and deluxe interiors. I remember calling customers to say that we had a car that came in and apologizing that it was not the one they ordered, and they'd still say that they would be *right down* to pick it up. Production was driving sales. Either customers would take what the factory dished out, or they'd tell us to give it to the next person on the list. One man with the patience of Job waited six months to get a 6-cylinder car.

One of the other Hudson dealers I got to know was a man by the name of John Placko. He had come over from the Old Country—living by the sack full of potatoes and brown paper bag just as so many immigrants from the century's early years had done, including my own family. John subsisted, became a mechanic, and finally landed a Hudson dealership. His two sons worked in the parts and service departments of the dealership which was then called

Placko Motors. (Both his sons are still in the car business today.) When a Hudson wreck would come in, the parts department would peel off all the chrome, the stainless steel strippings, and door handles, and hammer out all the tiny bends or tapers. Two hours would be spent with a ball-peen hammer restoring a dented hubcap worth maybe $2 new in those days. The staff would hang up used door handles on strings at the parts department, and sell them at half-price. That was their profit formula. Strictly odd-lot and small-ticket. Mine was to sell the big ticket in the highest volume. They were honest, hard-working people; but their business philosophy was different.

Because of our rapid growth, it was clear that I had to have a bigger showroom. I also thought that my prospects would be better on the North Side rather than the south because that's where the growth seemed headed. About a year after I opened in Chicago Heights, John Placko wanted to sell his store. My money was all tied up in Chicago Heights. But, while John didn't know it then, I already had backing to buy his Chicago store. Placko Motors was selling about 30 new Hudsons a month, but you could hardly believe that the dealership was open, let alone in the new car business. The front door of the dealership was *locked* and there was *one* car on a showroom floor that had space for five. John and Hudson were parting ways. He had been awarded a Studebaker franchise, and he was going to build himself a lavish dealership showroom in the old neighborhood.

Placko Motors was located at the intersection of Grand Avenue (running northeast), Central Park (diagonally), and Division (running northwest). The official address was 3569 West Grand Avenue. In many respects, it was not a good location and hard to find; but it was big, and there was room to grow. It remained the site of my dealership throughout the remainder of my Chicago days.

Before I signed the deal, though, two big questions had to be settled: What did the property cost and what would the terms be? We settled on a package of $110,000—that included parts, the one building (10,000 square feet), all the service tools (such as lifts, jacks, and floor creepers) and five used cars. John offered me a 30-year mortgage at 4.5%. I asked, "Can I pay this off in advance?" He inserted a clause allowing me to pay it off whenever I wanted at no penalty and even to extend the mortgage at the end of 30 years if I wanted.

What would I call my new dealership? For days, I mulled over two alternatives: Courtesy Motors and Guaranteed Motors. I liked Courtesy better because it symbolized the way that I wanted people treated; and, besides, it had a nice ring to it. That's the way I finally decided to go ahead, and I remember announcing the decision to my team during lunch at Paoella's Italian Restaurant over on Division Street.

In the new location, Hudson started me with the standard allocation of 30 cars a month. This was now 1948 and the War had been over for three years. Auto production was up and Hudson said that they could give me more cars. I was banking on it.

To his amazement, John Placko was paid in full one year later. Bewildered, he asked me if the factory had shipped me a lot more cars. I told him that the difference was we sold *used* cars. He thought that used cars were a bother and still believed that the money was to be made off servicing new cars in the back end, but that wasn't so. If they had spent more effort on used cars than reconditioned parts, this Hudson store could have made a lot more money for him and his family.

When the Korean War broke out in June of 1950, we knew cars were going to be in tight supply again; but the situation only lasted a short time, because the factories didn't convert to defense production. Not only did we purchase all the new cars that we could get (500 a month versus the 600 we asked for), we also bought up a lot of company fleet cars, used cars, and rentals in the anticipation that they would become more valuable. Hudson's General Sales Manager Jerry Hadley did the best to accommodate us—although so many of the cars were the same color, the shipments reminded me of the Model-T and a philosophy that dated back to the earliest Ford days and attributed to Henry Ford himself, when he said, "The customer can have any color as long as it's black."[c] Every new car was sold at full sticker. These market conditions lasted about six months.

The scarcities of cars and appliances actually became the makings of a very successful promotional event during this time. We offered car buyers their choice of a free major appliance when they bought a new car—appliances were still hard to get. To be able to come home with a new car *and* a new refrigerator in the same week was really something in those days.

Over the next 18 years, it's fair to say that we swallowed up a big hunk of the neighborhood. We started with 10,000 square feet and then we bought the Kaiser-Fraser garage next door and that added another 8,000 square feet. Next we bought a 10,000-square-foot factory that made Wonder Wash Auto Soap. Then we added other real estate including the next building—a machine shop called Grand Metal Forming Company. (It later became the Courtesy Conditioning Center.) That gave us altogether about 60,000 square feet.

On the back of the new space, we carved in some service stalls and a used-car lot. After that, there was no place to go but across the street. So we bought a bulk service station that stood on the corner and faced Central Park, Division, and Grand. Afterwards, we bought a coal yard which was about 90,000 square feet. (It was only worth $30,000, but it cost a quarter of a million. People were learning that I had a need for expansion and were taking advantage of it.) On it, I built a 100-car used car showroom. It was a very simple brick building paneled in wood instead of glass. In the summertime, we would just raise up the front and back doors and we would have a beautiful open exposure. These were specially made wooden garage doors—each 25 feet wide and 14 feet high—that had been converted into huge plate glass windows. Eight of these "window doors" lined the front of the used-car showroom. In the winter time, we would just keep the doors shut with a two-door entrance and had a huge, warm interior lot. We grew like topsy even though we were in a bad location. But later the power of television turned us into a true *destination*, and we needed every square inch that we could get. We ended up being spread over two city blocks.

We also started to do some car design tinkering on our own. That led to the saga of the Baby Hornet in 1950. The "Baby Hornet" was my first real customization of a factory-car line. The idea stemmed from my teenage experience at the Ford dealership, when the salesman described a Ford as a "Baby Lincoln". The Baby Hornet was my rescue plan for Hudson's Pacemaker. The Pacemaker was the Plainest Jane of the Hudson line. To sell it, I knew that we had to glamorize the car. I wanted people to feel that they were getting a stylish but economical version of the regular Hornet—Hudson's top six-cylinder offering.

Hudson was getting hot publicity from the successes of a Hudson stock-car driver named Marshall Teague.[4] We learned that Teague, in modifying basic models into race cars, took the flat cylinder head out of the cheaper Pacemaker and put it in *more expensive* Hudson models. The flatter cylinder head increased the compression, and the gear ratios were changed. On level terrain like that of Illinois, Michigan, and Indiana, this design worked fine and actually delivered better gas mileage. The first step in customizing, then, was to order the Pacemaker with Teague-style "overdrive" gear ratios, which we were able to do at no additional charge.

Next, the original recessed chrome taillights were scrapped and stored. An automotive magazine ad was the source for custom-made fin taillights we bought and mounted on the Pacemaker. This was the era when fins on the tails of cars became the rage. Maybe it was the result of the dawning space age and the fascination with rockets and jet planes. The

---

[4] Teague was later killed in an accident on the track.

new fins looked just like those on the Cadillacs but with three little chevrons added. Bob—our best lot man—spray-painted the taillight trim on a miniature assembly line over a work bench. The colors were genuine Hudson colors filled into spray cans at the local paint factory down the street. We ordered hood ornaments that were made for the Hudson "Commodore" model from the factory. (To this day, I still wonder what the factory thought we were doing with hundreds of extra Commodore hood ornaments.) We later customized the Super Sixes, too, in the same way and called a version of the custom package the Hudson Jetliner adding a thunderbolt symbol to the styling. We registered the name "Baby Hornet" and even had a stainless-steel nameplate pressed, attaching it to the trunk with stainless-steel screws. We patented this customization package and offered it for sale to every Hudson dealer in the United States. The price was $195, but no other dealer ever bought one.

We put our Baby Hornet invention on TV. (I'll talk about our television advertising program in just a bit.) Our dealership's ads for the Baby Hornet made everyone assume that you could find a Baby Hornet at *any* Hudson dealership. During the televised Hudson wrestling show, one of the announcers asked Mr. Teufel, another Hudson dealer with a store on Lawrence Avenue, if he handled the entire Hudson line. He said "yes, yes." The announcer ran down the Hudson line and ended: "Including the 'Baby Hornet', too?" Herr Teufel nearly had a heart attack. "Zer ees no such ting as a Baby Hornet!!!" he boomed. Teufel, of course, means devil in German. In effect, the "old devil" gave us a lot of advertising because we had Baby Hornets buzzing all over.

A little imagination let us create a whole new car concept. We sold Hudsons that the factory didn't even know they were "making." All in all, we sold more Hudsons than anybody—thirteen percent of the entire factory's output. The next year Hudson Motor Company came out with a Hudson Jet in their *own* lineup of new cars. When they

brought it to market, they didn't even know that I had registered both the names Hudson Jet and Hudson Jetliner. I
agreed that they could use the name Jet without charge,
except for a token one-dollar bill.

During the early fifties, a serious offer came my way to
go to Detroit and to drop the dealership business for the big
action of the Motor City. My "suitor" was no less than Henry
Kaiser. Henry Kaiser of Kaiser Aluminum had built the Free-
dom Ship Troop carriers during World War II. Kaiser's first
claim to fame was being one of the engineers to collaborate
in the building of Boulder Dam. After the War, he launched
the Kaiser-Fraser automobile operation, which started making cars in 1949. Howard "Dutch" Darien designed them.
One of them was called the Kaiser, and the other was called
the Fraser. Joe Fraser was the automobile man in the duo.
Henry Kaiser was the celebrated executive and financier.

Kaiser-Fraser's cars weren't selling. One Monday morning
in 1951, I got a call. It was Henry Kaiser himself—whom I
knew only by reputation. He told my secretary that he and his
son Edgar had just checked into the Drake Hotel and wanted
to come out and see me. I said sure. About 45 minutes later, a
big stretch limo pulled up in front. (Henry Kaiser probably
couldn't get a Kaiser or a Fraser from the rental agency!)

"Jim Moran," he said, "you're the most successful car
dealer in the United States. I wanted to meet you and ask
you about your ideas for our cars, because our dealers are
having a tough time." The Kaiser was a car assembled out of
components: It had a Lycoming engine, a "Detroit" transmission, Bendix brakes; and the styling (fair, not great) was
by the Frenchman Raymond Loewy. Still most cars were
selling then because of the shortage. I launched right in and
gave him a complete critique of his auto business. He said to
his son: "I want this man to come to Detroit and head up
our Kaiser-Fraser division." The senior Mr. Kaiser was 69.
His son Edgar was roughly my age, in his early 30s. Henry
said that he would put me in charge of styling, promotion,
and marketing, but I'd have to move to Detroit. Then he

said very slowly, "We'll pay you *$75,000* a year," which was a lot of money back then; but he said it as if he were offering me the world.

I told him it was a tremendous honor and I was very flattered, but I didn't know how good I'd be in a corporate job such as that. Then I told him that my dealership made $75,000 *over the previous weekend.* He was aghast. "What do you mean *over the weekend?*" he asked. I explained that we had sold over 300 new and 250 used cars and financed 95 percent of them and had made $75,000 easily. Over the average month, we were earning about $200,000 to $250,000. Our staff had grown to 300, and you could find 1700 new and used cars on our lot at any given time.

He went on though and said, "Think of the *prestige* you would have..." "Mr. Kaiser, you can't support my family on prestige," I countered. "It really doesn't mean anything to me. I like what I'm doing in the retail business." His son called me a couple of times after that, when their production fell to about 40,000 vehicles a year and their dealers were going out of business. In fact, the reason that we were able to buy the fourth building down the street to add to Courtesy was that the building housed a Kaiser-Fraser dealership. Finally, the Kaiser-Fraser auto business was disbanded.

Henry Kaiser was a large man—rough-hewn and street smart. But, on this venture, he was in over his head. Few people appreciate the sheer magnitude of the automotive business. I don't believe Henry Kaiser did—for all his street smarts—and I doubt that I did myself. A sadder but wiser Henry Kaiser later said of his interlude in the auto industry: "We expected to toss $50 million into the automotive pond, but we didn't expect it to disappear without a ripple."[d]

What caused some of the weaker automotive brands like Kaiser, Studebaker, Nash, Packard, and ultimately Hudson to fold was a two-part change in the industry. First, the Big Three were becoming extraordinarily powerful. And second, the other entrants were losing sight of their own real value. The new post-War realities and the increasing availability of product should have been a wake-up call, but some auto makers just weren't listening. Here's just one case: At the unveiling of the 1953 model in the Masonic Temple in Detroit, Hudson proposed a staggering increase in its list price. They actually felt that they could put Hudson in the same price class as *Cadillac*. I suggested that they do something about the pricing, or they would be out of business very soon. Other dealers no doubt complained too, because the prices were rolled back.

Relying on our own common sense, Courtesy Motors still managed to hang on to a salesforce of over 100 people in the 300-person staff, and you couldn't drive them away. The salespeople knew how to make money on both new and used cars. Some of our salesmen made $60 or $70 thousand a year—right up there with a surgeon of the time with a good practice. And, an average-to-good salesman might still have made at least $10 or $12 thousand a year. We may have fired a few for stealing or curbing a car, but we never had a salesman quit.[5]

> *"When I first started working for Jim Moran, I hadn't met him personally. We needed some fork-lift trucks, and I thought that I should run the order by him. He told me that he didn't know anything about fork-lifts. 'You decide. You go run it,' he said. Jim Moran gave a person the opportunity to do the business you were responsible for."*
>
> *— Bob France*
> *Retired Vice President*
> *and Parts Manager,*
> *SET*

---

[5] Curbing a car means bringing a neighbor's or a friend's car to work, parking it a block away, and then offering that used car as a "fresh cream puff in trade." The "curber" walks a prospect down the street, completes the transaction, handles the papers through somebody else, and then splits the profit with the owner. A curber would milk a dealer's advertising and reputation and could probably double his personal take on each deal until they were caught.

Every morning, we held an eight o'clock sales meeting. The day before we would pick two new car salesmen to hold "class." "Jack" would be told that he would speak about the quality of the door. Jack would spend five minutes on how well the door is hung, its safety, balance, trim, appearance, ease of locking, and window operation. "Bill" would be Mr. Bumper that day and describe the strength of the front bumper in another five-minute digression. Each day, I'd pick two different people and two different features to explain.

The speakers would talk about the chrome alloy block, the dual braking system—hydraulic or mechanical reserve, Step-Down design, or the fluid clutch. *The presenter was sharing the heart of a product-oriented sales pitch with all the other staff members.* Our sales pitch emphasized *product* because our product—the Hudson—was not accepted, and we couldn't evade perceptions. We had to confront them and to put our best foot forward. Let's face it: A car like the Pontiac was better looking, better engineered, better painted— almost better everything. We had to sell the customer on the advantages of the dual-braking system, step-down design, twin carburetion, fluid clutch (that never needed relining), more economical gear ratios, and an integrated body and frame.[6]

We would keep a tilted car mounted on the sales floor. The salesman would use a pointer and go through the features and then take the prospect on a test drive over cobblestone and railroad tracks and a stretch of high-speed road (50-70 miles per hour). We would plan our test-drive routes to show off the Hudson. "You can take a Cadillac and pick any terrain, and we'll prove that this Commodore will out-perform it," was the closing line. You had to work a lot harder to sell a Hudson.

---

[6] Ironically, as car design has evolved over the years, both step-down design and the integrated body-and-frame have since become industry standards.

"The people who dig the well are entitled to drink the water."

— Japanese Proverb

To sell as many Hudsons as we did, a crack sales force was a necessity. Back in the forties and fifties, a Chicago dealer found having Italian- or Polish-speaking salespeople to be as valuable an asset as Spanish-speaking salespeople are in Miami today. The area in and around Chicago has the second largest Polish community in the world after Warsaw. One Polish salesman we had would billboard us on a Polish-language radio program that he would emcee. It attracted a fair number of customers. Another Polish-speaking salesman, Stan Wojic, was a very effective deal-maker for us.

We had the number-one Hudson salesman in the United States. His name was Lee Green. Lee was the best product salesman—bumper to bumper, floor to roof—that I've trained. Simply a great salesman, but you always knew when Lee was around. He would drive his colleagues to distraction because he was constantly bumming cigarettes; but Lee had a disarming, smooth style that people couldn't ignore. He would meet customers at the door and say: "How do you do? My name is Lee Green. Welcome to Courtesy Motors. May I have 10 minutes of your time?" He would walk around the showroom display car tilted on its side and read each of the twelve informational signs posted there, describing every Hudson feature down to the aluminized muffler. For the climax, Lee would pound on the front fender with his fist while he praised the thickness of the metal.

"Jim Moran kept drumming product knowledge, product knowledge. Back in the Courtesy days, it got to the point where I would stroll around the dealership, flipping salespeople silver dollars when they answered a product question correctly just to keep the team sharp."

— Harvey Rumsfield
Manager of Training,
SET

A salesman of a completely different style was an older man named Hy Zussmann. He was 55 when he started with us and an artist on the side. He might sell only one car a day, but Hy would work one deal all day long just as though he was putting strokes on a canvas.

TELL IT LIKE IT IS

"Kicking the Tires: Heads-Up Consumerism"

Let's say you're in the market for a car. How should you shop? What should you ask? How do you get a fair deal? After half a century of selling cars, here is the best advice I can offer to buy one:

Pick a quality product. Paying attention to the ads and auto magazines is a start. Studying independent surveys—such as those conducted by J.D. Power & Associates—is very valuable. Best of all: Ask friends who know about cars. Some new car makes always seem to be on sale. Be careful. Often there's no resale market for those cars, and you'll get a miserable trade-in allowance later. On a car like that, you'll get your deal now...but, you won't get one later.

Be tough when you watch or listen to an ad. An ad can be helpful, but think carefully about what you see and hear: Is it believable? What accessories and features are included for the price? How much money down? If it's a lease, what's the term and do you have any responsibility for selling the car at the end? A good ad answers more questions than it raises.

Before you shop for a car, decide what is important to you. Everybody has different needs from a car: roominess for toddlers, easy handling, acceleration, looks...the possibilities make for a long list. A senior—let's say from a retirement complex—is usually after durable quality and safety. Retired people may have the time, but they do not want to go back and squabble with a service manager. They especially want an economical, dependable, trouble-free car. Think about what matters to *you* most and tell any car salesperson you visit what that is right off the bat.

Find a reliable dealer. Ask your neighbors, friends, and relatives. Technicians running around in white lab coats might tell you which car has the better specs; but only people like yourself can tell you which is the better dealer. Often, you don't even have to ask. Word travels. From the gas-station business I learned that if a person *isn't* treated right, he or she will tell *everybody*. How many times have you heard: "I've had nothing but trouble with..." If they're treated right, they *may* tell people too. At synagogue or church or in the office or at a family gathering, somebody will say, "I was treated real nice. They said what they were going to do and they did it." The key question for a buyer is: Will the dealership be there to satisfy me *after* I buy the car? On the "birthday" a year later, a good dealer will check in with a phone call. That kind of confidence and appreciation from the dealer merits trust from the customer.

Ask: What does the dealer or salesperson drive? Sounds like a funny question, doesn't it? But, I think the answer says a great deal about both the car and the dealership. I still drive the bread-and-butter cars, and I believe in that as a principle. That way I stay in touch with what most customers buy. And, it says that I have faith in the product.

That means I usually drive a Corolla or a Camry. What about the Lexus? All things considered, the Lexus is the greatest car around, *bar none*. I love the car. We also own the biggest Lexus dealership in the U.S. But I have a job to do: To know the needs of the mainstream customer. Anyway, a Corolla or a Camry is hardly a hardship to drive. They're outstanding cars, and they now have many features introduced in the Lexus.

If you're buying a used car, know that you're buying the dealer as much as the car. A reputable used-car dealer will offer you either a full exchange privilege or a good warranty or both. You're paying for the car's condition and the use left in it. If you buy a used car, and it's not "right," the dealer should make it right. When you shop, should you bring your own expert along? Probably not. If you bring a mechanic with you, how is he or she going to know what's going to happen to that car in 30-60 days? Experts don't have microscopic eyes that can crawl inside the pistons. It may run OK now, but 15 minutes later it can break down. Nothing—including the best reconditioned used car or even a brand new car—is perfect. Only the Almighty is perfect. In an imperfect world, what you *do* need is a good warranty. These days, you'll be better off using your head to study the deal than by using your feet to kick the tires.

No doubt about it: It was TELEVISION that turned the Hudson days into a bonanza for Courtesy Motors. If there's one achievement I guess that I'm proud of, it was bringing television to dealership marketing of cars. In 1948, there were just a sprinkling of television stations in the United States. One of them was WBKB in Chicago. Most advertising executives, especially those at the big agencies, thought of television as a toy. And why wouldn't you, when you were staring at a screen that was generally 6-by-8 inches? The ad pros didn't see it as a tool that would lead to any audience recall. The first TV set I saw was in the window of a neighborhood music/appliance shop. Even then, the commercial potential looked enormous to me...to be able to show a car on television...to be able to sell 40,000 or 50,000 individual customers at once. I took to it...and it to me. From day one and for some reason, it was as easy for me to talk to thousands of people as to talk with one.

We were certainly the first dealer to market used cars on television, and one of the first—if not *the* first—to sell new cars in that way. I can remember Marty Herod selling vacuum cleaners with a strong push style on television. And there were comics pitching refrigerators and jumping inside of them. (Not very good role models for youngsters.) The ads were mostly slapstick and not believable. But a car was different. You could put a car into motion: You could see its lines...Let your eyes wander over the styling and the interior.

There's one behind-the-scenes person more responsible for the television marketing of cars than anyone else, and that's Hal Barkun. You can blame him for drawing me into television and all those long Courtesy TV ads. An articulate, quick-witted marketing pro, Hal looks a lot like Groucho Marx. He's been a loyal friend, trusted business companion, and kind of an older brother for me for more than 45 years as of this writing.

In 1948, the city's ad agencies had been invited to a commercial television demonstration at WBKB-TV. All but one agency walked out unimpressed. Only Hal and his partner *believed*. They could see the potential in the medium and sold a three-hour wrestling show for about $1,200 in commercial fees. Some early sponsors experimented with that show but didn't stick with it.

Hal was also the account executive of the Malcolm Howard Agency who represented the Hudson Dealers Association in Chicago. They spent the "princely" sum of $195 a week on advertising to promote all *40* dealerships. That works out to $4.87 per dealership every seven days, and it was for a midnight radio program! At the same time, the Association was charging each dealer $15 per car sold for advertising, and the money was just accumulating in an account. Remember these were the post-War years and dealers really didn't believe that they had to promote their business because cars were still somewhat scarce.

Hal approached the Hudson zone manager about sponsoring a television program. The manager explained that he was the custodian of the promotional funds but that he had no authority to spend the money. To get the money spent, Hal would have to meet with the Dealers' Association and earn their approval. The next Tuesday, Hal was invited to the Dealers' meeting to make his presentation.

Since the Hudson Dealers were rolling in money, the presentation was scheduled to follow an excellent lunch at the Hotel LaSalle. Hal's pitch took about half an hour, and he recommended an initial buy of three hours of television time a week. When he asked for questions, there was dead silence, and Hal stood there feeling like a dummy. Finally I got up and said, "I want to ask the rest of you, how many of you have a television set in your home?" Nobody did. I went on to say that I had a set and that, some day, television was going to be the greatest entertainment and advertising medium in the world. "We have all this money today," I warned, "but as soon as Chrysler, GM, and Ford finish converting their factories back to civilian production, Hudson will end up at the bottom of the pile. We should be spending now to create an appreciation for our product. We're crazy if we don't buy this proposal."

"The future belongs to those who prepare for it. We are preparing for a great future."

— The Philosophy of
JM Family Enterprises

They agreed—a little to my own surprise. The next hurdle was getting started. Nobody had the faintest notion of how we would advertise on this medium. The only broadcast background that we had was with radio. What were we going to do for three hours? Our best solution looked like the wrestling show that had just become available for sponsorship. The twelve Hudson dealers in Chicago agreed to sponsor wrestling at a cost of $1,200 a week over a 13-week contract.

We decided that the dealers would rotate through the wrestling show sponsorship in groups of five. I was on the Hudson Advertising Committee along with four others and we were the first to be on the air. We piled into a Hudson, drove up to the Civic Opera Building while the television camera captured our arrival as the first visual in the show, got out of the car, and rode up the elevator to the 48th floor studio arena for the first Hudson Monday night wrestling exhibition. Each dealer attending was to get a commercial between each bout, and we went down to the street to show the cars. No problem being there on time since we knew when each bout was supposed to end! Ben Fohrman[7] and Ray Winkelwerter were two of the first group of five, as was I. Hal says I was good. That's an exaggeration—but I do know that I was the only one who felt comfortable in front of the camera.

---

[7] Two of Ben's sons (who were also in Ben Fohrman's dealership) were later killed by an irate customer with a shotgun right on the selling floor. It was a tragic affair. A customer had a problem and didn't feel that he was being given a fair hearing after several visits.

"From the very first broadcast, Jim Moran took to the television medium like it was meant for him. Movie directors will tell you that the camera loves certain actors. The TV camera loved Jim Moran. He looked good. He talked right. He wasn't the least bit nervous."

— Hal Barkun
Retired Advertising Executive

Almost all of the other dealers lost interest when the 13 weeks expired. Finally I wanted to take on the whole show myself. Hal checked if the other dealers minded. They didn't. One called me a "crazy kid" for considering what I had in mind. I signed up for 13 weeks for $1,200 a week and went back to the store. I told Harvey Rumsfield the facts, "Harv, if I got the bill today, I couldn't pay for it because all our cash is tied up in growth or inventory. So we better sell a lot of cars!"

"Wrestling from Rainbow"—as the show was called—was moderated by Wayne Griffin. He'd call the falls and do the color. There was plenty of color to do. Gorgeous George would primp his hair and throw out little Georgie pins to the crowd. Dick the Bruiser looked like a rough-and-tumble night club bouncer with a crewcut. They called Jim Landos The Greek God. Two Germans—Hans and Max Schnabel—were the tag-team champions and real antagonizers. Verne Gagne behaved like an honest-to-goodness athlete. They were among the most famous ring celebrities. In the neighborhood I grew up in, I knew a kid named Billy Goelz who turned pro wrestler. He would often be matched against another excellent wrestler by the name of Walter Palmer. Billy was a straight wrestler. While the bouts were still fixed, at least there wasn't any theatrics or perfume spraying. These two would almost make you think that it was for real. The program was intentionally called an "exhibition" rather than a sporting contest, and there wasn't much effort to conceal the fixing.

What made wrestling so popular? People liked the action. Everything was so clear cut, it was easy for people to root for a favorite or to boo a villain. They liked seeing their nationality or personality type—a type to whom they could relate—mixing things up in the ring. Unlike boxing, the contestants were rarely seriously hurt. It was entertainment—a way to let off frustration. The villains were sneering rude gorillas. The heroes were clean-cut and handsome.

Throwing people over the top rope was commonplace. In those days the arena had wooden folding chairs. I remember one 300-pound wrestler landing in a lady's lap. I'm nearly certain that it *was* staged, but it was made to seem not. In any case, the chair broke. She hit the ground hard, and they took her out on a stretcher. I had to ad lib a commercial for eight minutes because we were now so far ahead of the "official" schedule we had been given.

One problem we had with the wrestling show was what to do with the intermissions. At each show, the emcee would interview patrons or wrestlers for about 18 minutes. But, we were told *we* could get those 18 minutes if we knew what to do with them. Well, we knew! We decided to run some used cars on camera in front of the Civic Opera building and to show these cars with prices. As the bout before intermission started, I would hurry down 48 stories in the elevator, put on my mike and then during the break describe each used car as it pulled up. Worked like a charm. And by the time these cars were back in our showroom, there would often be a line of people, some in pajamas, waiting to buy the TV cars.

We kept the wrestling show, but—since we were clearly successful with TV—we decided to expand to live entertainment programs as well. We did this on WENR-TV, presenting a show called "The Barn Dance." WENR was the ABC affiliate.[8] We had our own dance troupe, just like

---

[8] "The Barn Dance" show had earlier been on WLS radio for years. Everyone figured that if it worked on radio so well, the show would be an even bigger success on television. It was.

the June Taylor Dancers on network TV. As the emcee, I wore a cowboy outfit and a white hat, and we handed out stacks of black-and-white photos at the dealership showing me in this outfit. The color of the rest of the costume didn't make a difference since this was still the black-and-white era. Entertainers like Homer and Jethro, Minnie Pearl, and Arkey the Arkansas Woodchopper and other classic celebrities appeared on the show. If tapes existed of that show and you were to watch them today, you might take it for an early version of "Hee-Haw"; but, the weekly production budget was only $1,000. Many name stars appeared for nothing or next to nothing simply for the exposure it brought to their acts for other potential bookings.

Then we started to alternate "Barn Dance" with a variety show called the "Courtesy Hour"—similar to Ed Sullivan's show later. We wanted to create a television alternative to radio shows like Jack Benny and Bob Hope. Our mainstays on the Courtesy Hour were veterans of the vaudeville era, the "Orpheum Circuit." We had the spelling genius Professor Backwards and Professor Irwin Corey with his outlandish ties—one long and one short. In addition to the novelty acts, our guests included the likes of Eydie Gorme, Henny Youngman, and many other big names in the entertainment business. Carol Lawrence, then a dancer and later a movie star, actually met her future husband Robert Goulet on our show. I'll never forget that show, because I introduced him as Robert Gul'-let, and the switchboard lit up like the White House Christmas tree. When the cast from the Broadway show *Carousel* appeared, I called this musical Ca-rou-sal. For all the mistakes in grammar and pronunciation I made, people accepted me—mostly because I concentrated on being myself—a car salesman.

A movie studio came to WGN-TV, a third Chicago station, with a package of 100 movies to televise. These were full-length movies uncut and unchanged, just as they were shown in the theaters. The package had some wonderful movies like Hitchcock's "Jamaica Inn" and the original "A

Star is Born" with Fredric March and Janet Gaynor. We decided to be the advertiser. Our problem was how to get viewers to tune in our film at the starting time. Up until then, people went to the movies any time. You went in at the beginning, middle, or end. And, if you missed some of the film, you stayed for the next show, to see what you had missed. You couldn't do that on television. So, we advertised on the TV page of the newspapers to announce our film and its starting time, and urged viewers to tune in.

Sometimes you could resell the rights, but generally we set up a deal with one-time airings once a week for $700. Hal Barkun would travel to California about twice a year to buy movies. They usually ran 13 to a package—four good ones, five fair ones and four forgettable movies. The poor ones would come immediately, but you would wait an eternity for the hits. And sometimes you learned that the promoter never had the authority to release the good ones in the first place.

One time the film for Sunday never even showed up. It was Saturday and the only first-run film Hal could get to replace it was "The Maverick Queen" with Barbara Stanwyck. Hal pre-screened it. I didn't. Even though Hal thought it was a dog, there was really no choice but to use it. We aired it. On Monday night I called Hal up and asked, "*Where* did you get that movie?" He was embarrassed down to his toes, and I didn't even let him answer. "Hal, we did more business off that movie than any one in months. Get some more like that." And it was the truth. My biggest disappointment came later when we sponsored the first showing of "The African Queen" in Chicago and NBC put "The Treasure of the Sierra Madre" on against us—both with Humphrey Bogart.

For the average TV show we had three cameras and they were gigantic, heavy, and subject to breakdown. By the end of the show, only one might be working. We improvised often. Interestingly enough, the earliest operators were women. Maybe the upheavals in the workforce as a result of the War were a factor. Primitive equipment complicated the lighting. A technician would work on the lighting for a full two hours before showtime. Nothing was automated. A typical studio would be half the size of an average hotel room. Backdrops were made out of cardboard. The sets were as hot as a parched desert.

We would do a minimal amount of rehearsing. I would line up the cars in the order that they would appear and let the director and camera operator know what I wanted to do with each car.

As a dealer on the lot, I was also the quality control manager constantly opening the doors and trunk lids of used cars. I'd look at the engine, the glove compartment...everything. The behavior drifted over to my television role. In a way, *I was a quality-inspector spokesperson.* That, I believe, came across on TV.

There was another side to the non-advertising remarks, too. The audience identified me with the little segues and one-liners as much as with the ads themselves. Unintentionally, because of the novelty of television at the time, I was also becoming an entertainment personality as much as an advertising spokesperson. I was enough of a celebrity to be invited to appear on other shows and fund-raisers. A lot of public speaking invitations resulted. I did accept appearances for some of the charities including B'nai B'rith and Knights of Columbus, United Way, Heart Fund, the Cancer Society, Cerebral Palsy, etc.

They say we drew a bigger audience than anybody—Ed Sullivan and Milton Berle included. Maybe. I only know that we put on quite a show for $1,000 a week while Ed Sullivan enjoyed a weekly budget of half a million dollars.

At one time, we had three shows: Wrestling on Wednesday night, Friday night for The Barn Dance (alternating with the variety show every other week), and the movie on Sunday. At first, the cost of television was very reasonable. As it became more expensive, we dropped the wrestling. The Friday night show drove our weekend business. The Sunday show drove our weekday business.

The schedule was pretty demanding on me. The service department of the dealership opened at 7 AM. The sales department opened at 8 AM. Sales closed at 11 PM, and service had an evening shift that stayed open until 10 PM. I used to make the 8 AM meeting. Three nights a week, I wouldn't reach home till twelve or one. The wrestling show could go to 12 or 12:30 AM. Was I happy when videotape came along in the sixties, and I could tape shows in advance. Then you could tape a show and go away. Before, if the little red lights were on in the studio, you had to be there.

Sears, Roebuck—also based in Chicago—wanted me to be their TV spokesman. Their marketing man called me and offered me $25,000 a year. I told him that it was a great opportunity but I was already making a little bit more than that in what I was doing. I didn't talk about my income, because I knew my earnings would have been all over Chicago in a matter of minutes.

The cars we advertised looked great on television and were immediately gobbled up. After the last commercial on our wrestling program, for example, there was one final bout; but I think that some people tuned out by then. By the time we got back to Courtesy Motors, as I have already said, people were lined up at the dealership to buy the cars that they had seen on TV. Even though we always tried to draw our TV cars from a group of the most popular and desirable makes and models (so we would have several similar automobiles on hand), at the beginning, nobody wanted the many other used cars we had, they only wanted the television used cars.

So we brought all of our cars up to the television appearance and condition standard. The television advertising actually drove our marketing policy. What was originally a cosmetic touch for television turned into an operating standard, because no dealer before us had paid that much attention to the appearance and mechanical condition of a lot full of used cars.

Through television, our trading area expanded from a neighborhood to an entire region. Our signal beamed out about 175 miles. We had customers in four states—Illinois, Wisconsin, Indiana, and Michigan. Lake Michigan didn't register much interference. We sold more Hudsons in Indiana than all the Indiana Hudson dealers combined and almost as many cars as all the Hudson dealers in Michigan combined. Because of television, we became *regional marketers*. But, television also taught us to close deals on the spot and to prep and deliver the cars within an hour of the time that they were sold. Once people drive 50 miles to go some place, they've committed themselves to a 100-mile day. They wouldn't be sleeping on their decision and coming back the next day. With the advent of television, the era of neighborhood dealership loyalty grew to a close.

I priced cars for volume just as I had priced gasoline, and the market was beating a path to our door. In late 1949, A. E. Barit—then President and CEO of Hudson Motor Car—came to Chicago. He visited our dealership, and the two of us had lunch at the Illinois Athletic Club. Hudson was having serious problems selling more cars, and I had a suggestion that might boost sales. He wanted to hear it. It was a sliding range of rebates for dealers. The more cars a dealer would buy, the better price they would get. For instance, a dealer who sold 500 cars over twelve months would have $120 per car rebated at year's end. A thousand cars—$220, 2,000 cars—$300 a year per car, 4,000—$360 per car. This system would give all Hudson dealers the opportunity and the incentive to compete better with the other brands. The extra money could allow us to advertise more and offer better trade-in allowances.

Thirty days later, Courtesy Motors had a new contract spelling out the terms exactly as I had proposed them...and so did every other dealer in the United States. I filed the paper away for about the next five years without giving the agreement a second thought, and we collected the checks that our high-volume performance merited.

In 1954, during The Barn Dance Show, I had an acute appendicitis attack. The appendix almost ruptured. An ambulance rushed me to St. Francis hospital, and doctors operated on me that evening. It was not planned this way, but the very next day the Hudson dealers filed a massive antitrust suit against Courtesy Motors. We were the only dealer to reach three of the plateaus in the incentive rebate program. Because we did, the rest of the Chicago Hudson dealers sued us under the existing anti-trust laws for $9.8 million, an astronomical claim for business damages at the time. It would be comparable to a $90 million suit today, and it was computed on the number of cars that *they* alleged they could have sold if they had the same price advantages that we did, but they never sold the cars. The other dealers calculated the supposed value lost to them retroactive to the *first* new Hudson I sold.

I had a kinescope camera (an expensive[9] 16 mm film forerunner of videotape) set up in my hospital room to record a message. Surrounded by doctors and nurses and propped up on some pillows, I said, "The only mistake we made was selling cars too cheap. This action just proves that you get a better deal at Courtesy Motors. We're proud of that fact. We're the only dealers doing such volume. Therefore we can sell you a car for less money." Neither my appendicitis nor the timing of the suit was staged. Certainly the *honesty* of my message wasn't. The whole commotion made the headlines, but the case never went to court. The dealers dropped the suit after a year and a half.

The Hudson era, however, was clearly drawing to a close. George Mason bought out Nash-Metropolitan, beginning a chain reaction that was to spell the end of Hudson. Charlie Nash had engineered the valve-in-head engine for Buick. He

---

[9]The cost of kinescope was so high that kinescoping a show would have equalled the entire production costs of a single show. That's why we never filmed any of our shows from that era for posterity.

wanted somebody with drive to succeed him, and that was George Mason. Mason was a rare combination of an engineer and a financial expert. He was appointed by the New York banks to oversee Walter P. Chrysler in the evolution of Chrysler Motors. As president of Nash, Mason merged the company with Hudson to form American Motors in 1953. The next year was the last year of the Hudson. What was called a Hudson Commodore was actually a Nash with a Packard V-8 and an Ultramatic transmission. The car had two problems: The transmission would suddenly upshift or downshift...and even slip into reverse. When the transmission plant in Willow Run, Michigan, burned down, Hudson and Nash bought Dynaflow transmissions from Buick. The new transmissions were a weak component. The second problem with this hybrid Hudson was that it was a devil to start. Too many clouds in the sky could kick the humidity high enough so that the mere six-volt system couldn't crank up the flat-head V-8 engine.

At AMC, Mason also acquired Kelvinator and Leonard Appliances and Nash. In addition, Mason designed the first Rambler convertible, with a pull down top resembling a window shade. Mason was not a strait-laced corporate type. He would whiz around the Kenosha AMC plant on a little Italian motorbike. He was a visionary, truly dedicated to miniaturization—long before the VW "Bug" really took hold or Japanese compacts were a factor in the American market. In some respects, the Nash Rambler station wagon was a sporty little car. But the Rambler wagon was really too small to be an all-purpose station wagon, and the styling was flawed. The roof looked as though it had been mounted on the car backwards. Still, in 1954, over 50 percent of the Ramblers sold were cross-country station wagons. The two-door sedan, with modified grill and taillights, called the Rambler American, rounded out the line.

Overnight we had become an American Motors Dealer, and we could see the whole situation heading south. When George Mason died unexpectedly, George Romney—later a major political figure—took the cash-poor company over.

The Ramblers we got from Kenosha were so problem-plagued that some would have an "N" for Nash on the hub-caps rather than an "R" for Rambler. The country was in recession, and AMC put its emphasis on finance rather than technology. It wasn't long before AMC was simply Rambler, and Ramblers were all that people were buying from us; and the sometimes spotty Hudson quality standards—which now looked good in comparison—had totally vanished. Pretty soon I really couldn't sell a Rambler to a friend and have them come back.[10]

Still we were doing 15 percent of AMC's total volume. Seeing that we couldn't continue this way, I asked Herb Tousley who would be most interested in us: GM, Chrysler or Ford? Herb agreed with me that GM—on the strength of Chevrolet—was selling everything they could, and they didn't need us. Chrysler had some strong brands and dealers, but they were clearly the third player in the market. Ford, however, was being outsold by Chevrolet 4-to-1, and this was the battle for the traditional American automobile. Meat and potatoes. Ford needed me, Herb felt, to recover some of that market share. "Do it with Ford," Herb said; and I followed his advice.

If I had walked into the Ford offices out in Hegewisch, Illinois, the first secretary to see me would call somebody connected with a Ford dealership, and the dealers would lock arms and band together against me. I wouldn't have a chance. Herb agreed to be my intermediary and to drop into the Ford offices and tell them that I would be very interested in renewing a relationship and to explain why I couldn't pay them a visit, but maybe we could talk business over lunch in a private room at the Illinois Athletic Club. (Its pool had become my regular morning swimming hole.) Herb reported back that they were interested.

---

[10] AMC, of course, no longer exists. It was acquired by Chrysler at the end of the eighties. Chrysler especially wanted the Jeep nameplate.

Herb and I brainstormed to get ready for the meeting. I wanted a life-time franchise, no yearly renewals. Ford had never done this, but I had my reasons. I didn't want them complaining that I didn't sell enough fertilizer to their pick-up customers or using some other excuse to cancel me. (Believe it or not, pickup dealers used to sell fertilizer...and bags of de-icing salt, too.) Herb said I'd never secure a lifetime franchise. Since that was so important to me, I decided to try it and see how far we'd get.

When we met, I suggested my terms to the three managers—regional, zone, and district. During about two and a half hours of talking, I told them what I could do with the product and the service. Yes, I would put a new facade on the building and buy signs...do all of those things. Then I unveiled my franchise desire, putting it this way: "If a dealer is doing a good job, you renew them every year. You cancel the ones who aren't." Yes, they agreed. "So what's the difference between a lifetime franchise that you could cancel and a one-year deal?" After a pause, they agreed that there wasn't any difference, with "Well-if-you-put-it-that-way..." looks on their faces. Ford had their attorneys scan my proposed language and approve it. I signed one agreement. I never signed another. And we loaded our inventory of 220 AMC cars on tractor trailers and shipped them back to the factory.

It probably sounds like this period of my life was that of the determined young business tycoon, with one business deal or decision after another. In truth, I never saw it that way. Since my earliest years, the only thing I knew was to work hard; that's what I did. But, there was more to my life. During the fifties and early sixties, I was father to a young family of three children. After Kitch was born in 1943, Pat came along in 1945 and Jim Jr. in 1948. I shouldn't really talk about raising children, because I had so little to do with bringing mine up. They were usually asleep or at school when I got up. At night, they were generally in bed by the time that I returned home. My wife took care of everything related to the home. We *both* tried to set a good example by not smoking or drinking, attending church regularly, and generally trying to live a life involved in the community.

One evening ritual that we followed whenever I could be there was: ice cream. Ice cream has always been a passion of mine. After dinner, the kids would go down to the local dairy store and come back with a half-gallon. The "awful-awful" sundae we used to call it. We'd scoop up a sundae with bananas, hot fudge, marshmallows, butterscotch—everything but the kitchen sink.

Not wanting to expose the family to the attention I was now accorded as a "celebrity", we stayed home a surprising amount of the time. On a few of those nights when I got home early, though, we would go to Riverview—Chicago's answer to Coney Island.

We lived in a home in Lincolnwood with four bedrooms, four baths, and a three-car garage. It was built on three lots and cost $60,000—a pretty penny, I guess, for the time. Still, it didn't look all that special, except for the Olympic-sized swimming pool in the backyard.

And then there were the holidays. Christmas time in the neighborhood was a spectacle, and I mean that literally. It was back in the days when people mounted string upon string of lights and huge lit displays of Frosty the Snowman or Rudolph the Red Nosed Reindeer on their houses. People went all out, and the spirit of Christmas soon gave in to the spirit of competition. I remember nights when I would stand out in front of the house like a traffic cop waving on cars with sightseers so I could back out of the driveway to get to the station for a broadcast. One year, a neighbor close by outdid us all, and we knew that no one could ever hope to compete in the future. I mean, *how could you ever hope to top life-size Nativity statues with live manger animals—sheep, cows, and a donkey?!*

As for me personally, there were three hobbies that I made time for. One was Little-League baseball and the other two were swimming and boating. Jim Jr. and I found time on free summer evenings to play catch on our driveway. For seven years I coached Little League. Pat liked to tag along to Little League games and developed quite a knack for being the official scorekeeper. (Could that be why she's so good today reading the financial statements of JM Family Enterprises?)

Many of the Little League kids knew me as the guy they would fall asleep watching as they stayed up for the late-night movies on Sunday evening, and some even lasted until my "Good night and God bless you" signoff. To me, the most important thing was that the kids feel comfortable and enthusiastic and that they learn something from the experience, not that winning was the most important thing. One time, our team lost a close game because a kid named Ray Larsen—a terrific hitter—ripped the cover off of a fastball and put it out of the park. The truth is I should never have let our team pitch to Ray, and I told them it was clearly my fault.

I really enjoyed coaching pitchers. One of the best players I ever got to know in Little League was a fellow named Alan Chapman. Tough as nails. Although he was a pitcher, Alan was also a catcher—once. The ball broke through the web of the mitt and hit him so hard it nearly knocked him out. He didn't cry. He just got up and put some ice on the sore spot. Later that night, he played the entire game. Afterwards, I went over and congratulated him. I was the opposing coach in that game, but I even called Alan's father and told him how I admired his son. One thing I'm really proud of was the attitude that my son Jim took. Whether he was playing on a team that I coached or not, he would be very mature in avoiding even the appearance of favoritism, and we would both put the interests of the team above our relationship.

One of the best things about Little League was the chance to connect kids with solid role models. One of my favorites was Ernie Banks, a great all-around player for the Cubs and a leading hitter then, whom I invited to speak at a number of Little League functions. He really had an impact on the youngsters.

Auto racing never much interested me, but boat racing certainly did. We had a summer place in Johnsburg, Illinois, and I loved to race on the Fox River and actually competed in Class E races. For this class, the maximum length of the boats was 17 feet and the top engine size was 144 cubic inches with three carburetors and two cockpits—although the rule requiring a second cockpit was later dropped. These races were held on inland lakes like Channel Lake and Lake Geneva or on the Fox River. While I never won any major races, it was fun; but it was usually a mad dash from there to the studio on Sunday night to emcee the movie broadcast.

Of course, being a "car man", it was almost a sacred duty to teach my three kids to drive as they came of age. They all learned on a three-speed stick shift. When Kitch turned 16, she got her first car—an aqua Ford convertible—for her birthday. It was partly a present and partly a purchase with the savings that she had built up from her part-time work. She was beaming. When I asked her what she thought of it, she sort of summed up the family sentiment in one sentence: "Dad, I'm just so happy it's not a Hudson."

4

Torture Time

1955–1965

The new Ford agreement was signed, but even before I opened the doors of Courtesy Ford, my new dealer colleagues made it crystal clear that they didn't want me in the Ford dealer fraternity. Remembering my earlier Ford years and my sponsorship of the wrestling shows, people were calling this the "Grudge Match of the Decade." The other local Ford dealers banded together and sent a telegram to Henry Ford II, demanding that he rescind the decision to give me a dealership. There was a veiled threat that otherwise they might resign. Many were afraid that I would rekindle the competition and force them to go back to work. The truth is that they just weren't minding the store. The dealers threatened to come to Detroit if Henry Ford didn't revoke my franchise.

Henry Ford II was nearly as self-confident and outspoken as his granddad the original Henry Ford. Hank the Deuce[e] (as Henry II was sometimes called, by workers especially) told the Chicago Ford dealers to resign, and I give him credit for that. His position was that Ford needed better dealers like Jim Moran. It was a free country, he said, and he could cancel anybody as a dealer—especially with Chevy outselling Ford 4 to 1 while there were twice as many Ford dealers as Chevy dealers! Ford was digging its own grave through the sheer number of dealerships they created. The firm was the victim of a "one is good, two is better" philosophy. When I rejoined the Ford system, Ford had 42 dealers in the greater Chicago area! Ford cut the territories up into such small pieces that the dealers couldn't make a profit. The closest rival Ford dealership to me, for example, was a mere one-and-a-half miles away.

To open business on May 1, 1955, the Ford people told us that we could order anything we wanted. So, Ted Scheml, the car distributor from the district office in Melrose Park, came to the store and spent a day with us. At an internal sales meeting in April, I said that I wanted to sell 1,000 new Fords in the first month. We actually sold 1,017 new Fords at retail in the first 31 days.

> *"The night Dad got the Ford franchise, we drove around the neighborhood with him in a Ford and tried to spot how many Fords there were versus Hudsons. We kids had thought that Hudson was so 'uncool.' It had no 'class.' We told him, 'Dad, you're on the right track.'"*
>
> — *Arline "Kitch" McNally*
> *Director,*
> *JM Family*

In those first years of my return to Ford, Country Sedan and Country Squire station wagons "with wood" were popular sellers and substantially better than the Rambler wagons we had been selling. We were able to quickly transfer the reputation and loyalty of the Courtesy Dealership to a totally new product. Customers who were loyal to the dealership were frankly thankful that we weren't selling Hudsons and Ramblers. The Ford models of the next three years helped, too. The '55 Ford was a smash. The '56 was even a little better. And, the '57 was fantastic. But, many dealers termed the '58 a "dog" from front to tail.

Instead of having steady, continuous quality from year to year, each fall unveiling brought us to a styling-and-engineering "roulette table"—with dealers in the field waiting for what Detroit dreamed up. In those years, Ford listed at $100 more than Chevrolet, model for model. Yet, a year-old Chevrolet had $300 more resale value than a comparable Ford. Buying a Ford almost automatically put you out $400 in a year.

The reason for Chevy's dominance was simple: Chevrolet came out with the overhead-valve Kettering engine in 1955, its first V-8. The '56 and '57 Chevrolets were very peppy cars with their hydraulic valve-lifters and automatic transmissions. GM was the enterprising automaker with knee-action coil springs, great chrome and paint jobs, highly styled interiors, advanced transmissions, and hydraulic brakes. Shut the door and you'd hear a nice thump; shut the door on a Ford and everything trembled. Ford still had the old push-rod engine. Their valve-lifters needed constant adjustment. The Fordomatic transmission whined and howled. The quality was missing, and the home office refused to innovate—holding on to the same V-8 for 20 years. As a result, a lot of folks—as the late Dinah Shore sang—were seeing the USA in their Chevrolet.

In 1958 Ford thinned every piece of metal on the car. Our service manager would shake the car from side to side, and you could see that even the wheels flexed. Chevrolet really took advantage of Ford's manufacturing weakness. The '58 Impala Coupé took the best parts of the Oldsmobile Rocket and the best parts of Cadillac and put them together. It was beautiful, and sold the pants off us. We got advance word about what was coming from Chevrolet in 1958 and tried to alert Ford through their district management, but they ignored us.

On one of our Michigan visits, we saw other evidence of Detroit's woeful manufacturing quality at the time. Dealers and managers were invited to the grand opening of the new Lincoln-Thunderbird assembly plant in Wixom, Michigan. It was a gala affair which included a tour of the assembly plant in operation. We got a revealing behind-the-scenes look. To fit the hood properly, four strong men wearing heavy gloves would bend open the hood and align it into the space between the front fenders. If the alignment wasn't exactly right, a fifth man with a padded baseball bat would actually whack things into shape!

The 1959 Ford Flip-Top convertibles offered a whole new body style plus hard tops that opened and closed at the touch of a few switches. Well, almost open and closed. There were too many solenoid switches—32—that all had to collaborate at once. First the trunk went up, and then four more switches loosened the top itself, four more flipped the top over and back. And so forth. If one switch didn't work, the whole system shorted out. No doubt, the car would have been much better built with today's electrical engineering and microprocessors than with what was available back then. Still, I felt that I had to defend the brand on television. One day we filled the entire showroom with these Flip-Tops and went on camera *live*. On a signal, this entire chorus line of Flip-Tops dropped their roofs at once. And luckily they all worked!

Despite the "flip-top" follies, 1959 was a good year for Ford, but the 1960 model was a tough sell. The high quality of the 1959-design body concept was abandoned, and the two-seat Thunderbird was dropped. Both decisions were mistakes. We went to the grand announcement of the 1960 Ford in Detroit. But the splashy unveiling wasn't backed by any true innovation. Ford had simply taken the Mercury body style and clamped the Ford nameplate on to it after making a few minor changes to the grill and tail-lights. Still, the change was jarring for loyal Ford customers—a real departure from the square body styles of the previous years. Even the Ford people in the field disliked the new look.

At an early age, with my parents and older sister.

C. W. Pfister   R. L. Millar   M. S. Holmes   J. N. Felten

J. R. Moran   D. J. Murphy   F. J. Gaughan   J. C. Clements   R. L. B...

About the only thing of practical value I learned in high school was Latin. It helped my public speaking later. (My picture is first on the left in the bottom row.)

Study the windows of the Hudson Dealership and you'll see that
"As Advertised on Television" was our big claim to fame.

Harvey Rumsfield (left) and I on camera during a car ad in our early television years.

Herb Tousley — who recently passed away at the age of 94 — from the Hudson days forward, a loyal and trusted business adviser.

"Courteously Yours"
Jim Moran

In the cowboy costume I would wear hosting the barn dance show. I don't know how many thousands of those autographed photos we gave away at the dealership. For some reason, people wanted them.

The Courtesy Ford dealership in 1959. We occupied about two square city blocks. Today the site houses Jewel Food and Osco Drug stores.

Calling do-si-dos on our "Barn Dance" program. We even had our own dancing troupe.

One of the swimming competitions we sponsored. Our biggest prize winner was Abdel-Latif Abo-Heif, a major in the United Arab Republic Army who was stationed in Alexandria, Egypt, and who trained on the Nile.

Our telethons attracted celebrities as diverse as the Harlem Globetrotters (below) and Wild Kingdom's Marlin Perkins (right).

"Oh Cisco!" "Oh Pancho!" "Oh Jim!"
At work for the American Cancer Society with
Duncan Renaldo and Leo Carrillo.

Congratulating
Hal Barkun,
my advertising guru
and the man who
first put me on TV,
after a successful
telethon for charity.

The Morans on the cover of *TV Today* (a forerunner of *TV Guide*). Jim Jr. is on the right. Kitch is sitting on the floor. Pat is on the left.

Pat Moran made her first TV appearance with me on the "Barn Dance" show in the early 1950s. Today, Pat is President of Southeast Toyota Distributors, Inc., and JM Family Enterprises, Inc.

Our Courtesy Used Car Guarantee. We were proud of how it revolutionized the industry.

Our Courtesy reconditioning plant was the first of its kind to overhaul used cars on such a vast scale, and our own quality standards
were frankly much higher than Detroit's originals.

Here I am with Bob Hope on a Cerebral Palsy Telethon. Perhaps the
most American of all entertainers in our century, and — wouldn't you
know it — Bob was born in London, England.

The first and only auto dealer ever to appear on the cover of *TIME* magazine. A combination of Gunsmoke's Matt Dillon, Liberace, and Bishop Fulton Sheen, *TIME* said. All I see is a cold guy in an overcoat.

Eiji Toyoda (left), honorary chairman of the board, Shoichiro Toyoda (center), Toyota's present chairman, and Tatsuro Toyoda, Toyota's current vice chairman — members of a distinguished family who have created the world's finest automotive business.

Shotaro Kamiya (left) went on to become Toyota's president. In Japan they revered him as *the god of sales*. Yukiyasu Togo (center) recently retired as chairman of Toyota Motor Sales, USA, and is a distinguished marketer as is his successor, President Shinji Sakai (right).

From the day Seisi Kato asked me "What would you do with 10,000 Toyotas?" and I said "Sell 'em," we were friends for life. Here we are together in Port Everglades in 1967.

A photo captured at our 25th anniversary celebration in Orlando.

Eiji Toyoda and I holding the Toyota Motor Corporation plaque presented on our 25th anniversary.

An aerial photograph of our Jacksonville Port and Processing Center.
Six hundred and thirty cars a day go through this facility.

Five hundred cars can be unloaded in a mere hour, and cars are allocated
to dealers by computer while the ships themselves are at sea.

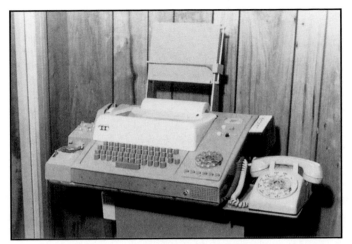

Our earliest "computer" — a Teletype 33 ASR. We were the first to computerize an auto distributorship.

One of our associates at World Omni Financial Corp. overseeing an optical disk scanner. In one minute, it can read and store 120 sheets of paper into digital memory and even smooths out any wrinkles in the papers all on its own.

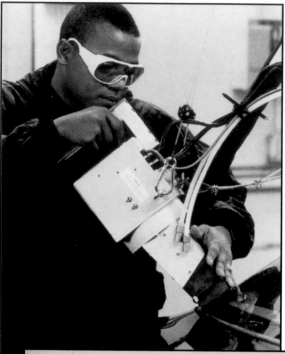

An associate etching a security number into the windshield of a new Toyota with high-tech laser equipment.

One of our traditional lunch meetings. We still have them today at JM Family.

At our 25th anniversary celebration, Squire Fridell and I, along with our wives Suzi and Jan. Squire and I are salesmen from two different television generations.

My wife Jan and I with probably America's most beloved entertainer, Bill Cosby.

Graduation Day at the
Youth Automotive
Training Center, the
most rewarding charitable
activity with which I've
been involved. We've
graduated 16 classes so far.
America's future...and I
think it's our responsibility
to back these young
people 100%.

Chi Chi Rodriguez is one of
the nicest and most successful
professionals in the world of
golf today and a tremendous
supporter of programs for young
people.

My wife Jan and I with Dr. Melvin Stith, Dean of the
Florida State University Business School and a member of the YATC board. Dean Stith is a brilliant and
caring leader. He impressed us so much that we
founded an Institute for Global Entrepreneurship
at Florida State.

My wife Jan is a wonderful
partner to me and a great asset
for our company in her
management of our marine and
aviation fleets and other areas.

Jan and I with our Labradors
Misty and Babe.

Aboard the *Gallant Lady*, a step up from streetcar
society on Chicago's Near North Side.

Pat and I together.
We have a great future, and Pat will take us there.

I requested a personal audience with Ford's President Robert McNamara in the corporation's ivory tower. When he asked me how I liked the new car, I said that it was terrible looking and that I couldn't understand why the change had been made. McNamara protested that we were giving the public a Mercury at a Ford price. "But, who wants a Mercury?!" I countered. In used-car lots, Mercurys were selling for less than Fords. Mercury never really caught on. As a retailer, I considered a Lincoln-Mercury dealership a tough option. As for the two-seat Thunderbird, Ford contended that they had broken up all the manufacturing dies (which I didn't believe) and that the car was really not a strong seller (which I didn't accept either). The quality improvements that were attained in 1959 were largely erased in 1960 when Ford tried to improve its bottom line through cutting costs.

Robert McNamara was a well-meaning, factory-type executive—who later went on to become Jack Kennedy's Secretary of Defense—but he was an intense cost cutter. In the new body style of the '60 model, the hood, wheels, and door channels suffered from poor quality. Ford also economized considerably on the front compartment—carpeting, pedals, pedal covers, and kick panels—and you could tell. Nothing a dealer could do could correct the 1960 car's construction and engineering problems.

Although Edsel was Henry Ford I's son, everybody laughed at the Edsel name as a car brand. In his own right, Edsel was a fine executive who had bad problems with his father, who was a bona fide tyrant in his later years. With all due respect for Edsel Ford the person, Edsel was a clumsy, unappealing name for a car. If the name wouldn't have killed the Edsel, the horse-collar grill would have. When I looked at the car at the previews in Detroit and heard that it was to be a step above the Mercury and would be a separate franchise, I tallied up property, building, parts, signs, and all the other overhead costs of an Edsel dealership in my head. The idea didn't make economic sense. Here was a car that would

cost more than the Mercury. Still, it was on a Mercury plat-
form. So what was different? All that was different was the
appearance, and the styling they offered failed. It was simply
a poorly designed car...and a quarter-billion-dollar mistake
for Ford.[f] The Edsel only stayed on the market between
1958 and 1960, and the line was ultimately retailed through
Lincoln-Mercury.

I passed on the Edsel, just as I had passed on the
Tucker—but the Tucker was probably a better car. Preston
Tucker had taken over a war plant in Chicago. His dream
was to build a revolutionary car.[g] The model he came up
with had a Cyclops-eye placed below the hood and headlights that would pivot in their housings. If the wheels
turned, the headlights turned. Rear-engine, water-cooled,
aerodynamic, and very good looking.

Tucker wanted to give me 300 cars a year—a big commitment for him at that time. The franchise would cost
$50,000 with a bonus of free luggage when you signed up
for the first car. People were telling me to do it. But I was
skeptical. Where was it going to be built? I walked
through the factory site; but where were the overhead
cranes, benches, and assembly line tracks? Nonetheless,
Tucker did build about fifty cars. Some friends of mine
spent thousands, but all they recovered out of it was the
luggage.

Still, I believe that Preston Tucker was a sincere man
with revolutionary ideas. With equal candor, he didn't have
the tools, dies, people, or engineers to get the job done. To
me—and to others—it looked as though the Big Three froze
him out.

During the fifties, all kinds of potential distractions
arose for me: Henry Kaiser, AMC, the Edsel, Preston
Tucker. But what about the meat-and-potatoes Ford business? Ford's quality bobbed around during the early sixties
but the quality trend was generally toward the better. It
wasn't until the fall of 1963 that Ford truly put it all together. It was then that the 1964 Ford Mustang was launched.

What a car. Ford's Vice-President and General Manager at the time, Lee Iacocca deserves the credit for the Mustang. By 1966, a million Mustangs were sold, and a great many of those rolled off of the Courtesy Ford lot.

By the early sixties, our dealership had become something that was, until then, unknown in the history of automobile retailing. We ceased to be a small business and started to be a big one. If we were to succeed, we needed to revamp our communications so that we could stay in touch with the issues. The way we kept things together was as basic as you can get. In a word, it was called: lunch.

At Courtesy Ford, lunch was more a management tool than a meal. I had a kitchen put in to end the distraction of going out to lunch and essentially to let us keep our finger on the pulse of the business—what's going on in parts, sales, used cars. It was a forerunner of the Quality Circle. Ford headquarters would have daily executive lunches too. But any production change costing over 12 cents a car went directly from the free discussion of their dining room to the gridlock of committee review. If you want to keep things moving, you must be prepared to make decisions then and there...and go on to the next thing.

Lunch continues to be the center of my business day. We eat and chat for 30 minutes, and we may talk really serious business for an hour more. Mostly the lunches have no set agenda, but we do have constant follow-up to make sure things are handled. We don't take notes. Few memos are written. We stagger attendance. In fact, sometimes I'll shake things up and ask that 10 Associates at different levels board one of our jets and come down from Jacksonville or Mobile and have lunch with us. Department heads pick some attendees on a rotating basis, and representatives brief others in their respective department. In fact, spin-off luncheon meetings are happening throughout JM Family every day. The philosophy is simple: I've always felt that it's better to have a two to three idea lunch than a two to three martini one.

"Jim Moran listens 'til he gets a headache. He's an incisive listener. That's what happens at those luncheon meetings still today. It's the listening that makes them so effective."

> — *Bill Donohoe*
> *Retired Vice President,*
> *Governmental Relations,*
> *JM Family*

During the Ford days, we really learned some crucial things over lunch. For example: the sales potential of the fully equipped car. We decided to have one car on the showroom floor loaded with every accessory and option possible. Funny thing: I first expected such a car to be there for at least a month. It turned out that it would be gone the next day! A lot of people—it seemed—wanted a fully equipped car.

As a Ford dealership, we had about 200 customers on a special program that some have called the forerunner of short-term leasing—an alternative that has become so popular in our industry today. Every year, for $650, they would get a brand new car, similar series—similarly equipped. If they had a Ford Sunliner convertible with automatic transmission, power steering, power brakes, and electric windows, next year they could get one for $650. There was no catch—provided that the car came back with less than 12,000 miles, which was very fair for a year; and the car couldn't have any dings, dents, or nicks. It had to be a nice, clean, ready-to-go car.

"In 1987, Yukiyasu Togo challenged Mr. Moran to find a way in which Southeast Toyota could be a leader in the United States in customer satisfaction as well as in sales. Jim Moran guided us to the answer—an answer we achieved—and the answer was balance."

> — *Dave Majcher*
> *Vice President,*
> *Service*
> *SET*

These 200 folks would come in during August and maybe change their color preference or request a different interior. Their order went off to the factory immediately. I knew that they would maintain the car and not reset the odometer. They were *custodians* of the car and because of income or position they gave status to the nameplate and most of all to the dealership. It was also like sending out a fleet of unbeatable word-of-mouth marketing spokespersons every fall. They felt pampered and inevitably told five or ten of their closest friends. The multiplier was enormous in drawing other buyers to Courtesy. Another thing that helped establish customer loyalty was truly paying attention to people. Something as simple as remembering who they were and what they bought.

> *"No one is more effective with people one-on-one than Jim Moran. And, that's what the JM Family company has become—a network of finely tuned one-on-ones that just keeps growing every day. It's a tradition begun by Jim and continued by Pat today."*
>
> *— Bob Barnett*
> *Williams & Connolly*

By the way, you don't have to have a great memory to remember people in our business. When customers visited us, we made it a point to complete "UP" cards with their name, address, and home and business phone numbers. (Similar 5 × 8 cards are still used by our Toyota dealers today.) The cards also contained a lot of other important information such as what prompted the customer to visit the store.

At Courtesy Ford, we had turned used-car retailing into an art. Our warranty was unconditional and iron-clad. It covered the tires, the brakes, the lights, the electrical accessories. People simply weren't cheated. *We've taken the fear out of buying a car* was my message on television and I meant it. We set a new standard of expectation. Take the car to any mechanic you want, I would tell the viewers. Anything that they find wrong with it, we'll fix. Other dealers disliked me for a 100 percent unconditional guarantee on the car with no charge for parts or for labor, for 30 days or 4,000 miles, whichever came first. Some dealers would claim it wasn't real. We'd show our guarantee on TV, and the camera would dolly in as I read it aloud.

> *"Having had the chance to watch Jim Moran manage his business over the past couple of years, I find that he exhibits great personal leadership and I admire him for his tenacity and ability to get things done. He is a true leader of his company."*
>
> —*Carl Cannon*
> *Publisher*
> *The Florida Times–Union, Jacksonville*

The most important thing about selling a used car hasn't changed. It is financial and not mechanical: What car price will the bank accept for financing? The customer must like the car, but it must also be financeable. Customers' dreams sometimes outstrip their wallets. It's both educating them and building confidence in our specialized knowledge. If you were to look at a present-day example, some customers will want a '94 Camry when they can really afford only an '91 Corolla. The salesperson has to bridge the bank's expectations and the customer's desires. In any used-car operation I've run, I've always done my best to train the salespeople to make a realistic match between the car and the customer's budget.

Back in the fifties and sixties, the Courtesy Conditioning Assembly Line reconditioned as many as 800 cars a month. It made its own white-wall tires, very popular then, with molds for three different sizes. The plant had two big commercial steam cleaners that could run 24 hours a day. Each car would move from stall to stall for each step in the reconditioning process—brakes, generators and starters, motor tune-up, transmission and differential, tires, batteries and electrical accessories—with the last stage being the final cleanup. The staff would wield toothbrushes to clean the last nooks and crannies. We bought upholstery fabric *by the semi*, and six specialists with sewing machines stitched together the fabric.

Our volume position allowed us to open up entirely new market segments including luxury used cars and imports.

We sold more used Cadillacs in Chicago than any other dealership. The factory-owned stores wholesaled them to us. Our mechanics were so good with Cadillacs that we even improved the pulley shafts of one model with a high-tensile steel bolt of our own design because the original factory part strained from too much of a load. Our luxury auto business was run by "Ollie" Lewis, who was a distinguished, soft-spoken gentleman in his sixties. Ollie had sold his Chrysler-Plymouth dealership on Devon Avenue and wanted something to do. So we created a Luxury Car Department and made him the manager. Its showroom had luxurious red drapes and special lighting. We sold a vast number of Cadillacs but stayed away from the used Lincolns because nobody wanted them. Cadillac was certainly the standard-setter among American makes back then.

We started importing in about 1955, and we actually became the largest import retailer of cars in the United States. People had confidence in us, even though we only had room to display five new cars of any make on the showroom floor at any one time. Some imports offered great prices, but we all wished that their quality was better.

Our first real import commitment was to the Triumph, which we began offering in 1958. What was the attraction? Most of all, the car was very reasonably priced. We brought them over by the boatload. We offered the TR-3 Roadster and the successor models, the TR-4, TR-5, TR-6—all of them two-seat sportscars. The TR-10 was a sedan, two-door or four-door. The Triumph was definitely a "price car." It was so small—"roller skate" size. We paid under $500 a car and sold them at $995, but a Triumph started only with great difficulty when the first autumn leaves fluttered off the trees because there was no pump on the carburetor. We could sell as many as 90 a month and were the brand's leading American dealer at one point.

We sold more used VWs than any Chicago VW dealer. The auto-design genius Ferdinand Porsche was actually the person who thought up the concept of the VW before World War II. The VW was an image or a "theme car". Kids loved the car. Contrary to common belief, the quality wasn't very good. The Beetle was noisy and troublesome, and certainly not roomy. VW customers wanted low price and economy, and they got it. VW made advances because they had a good distributor and dealer network behind the car.

In 1961, we became the number one Renault dealer in the US, but replacement parts such as water pumps were a nightmare to get. We didn't handle Renaults for long. They were 4-door sedans with an air-cooled engine in the trunk. The Renaults weren't the sturdiest make around, and I suspect that we made some enemies with the car. We tried Peugeot but dropped the line when we found that we could only get a limited number. Peugeot had somewhat better quality than Renault, but the make was not worth two times the Renault price.

The Jaguar was another import experiment, but we found it to be much overrated. We kept a battery charger on one model all the time, because of the dead shorts in it. A beautiful car, but poor mechanically. We handled the Jaguar, Jaguar XKE, the Jaguar Saloon and the Coupé. They were all troublesome, and it was hard to get parts. The XKE would sell for $4,500 or $5,000, but if you blew a clutch the dealer would have to have a Royal Air Force Spitfire fly one in from the UK! Nonetheless, the Jaguars and Triumphs were our main import business during the 1960s.

Our most distinguished import, though, was a used Rolls Royce—just one. Harvey Rumsfield bought a Rolls

Royce one day, and we put it on television. In rapid fire, there were three deposits on the car and the gentleman who owned Turtle Wax came in and paid the full advertised price for it in cash. Harvey bought it too cheap and he sold it too cheap, as he will readily admit.

The story of Courtesy Motors would be incomplete without an account of Courtesy Service's Grand Opening.

After some time, Courtesy's business had grown so much we felt that we should make a special effort to sharpen our customer service. After a great deal of discussion, we decided to build a special service facility to take care of our customers. Its Grand Opening would take place on the afternoon of our Sunday Night Courtesy Theatre, and we advertised the event on our television shows and in large ads in the newspapers.

We expected a few hundred visitors. Some optimists said we would get a thousand. But nobody anticipated what actually happened. By early Sunday afternoon, people began to arrive. Not hundreds, but thousands! There wasn't a parking space in the whole neighborhood. There were people crowded in our new car showroom, in our used car showroom, and especially in our new service facility. A full orchestra played tunes as we served cake and coffee; and big name stars sang their hits, danced, and told stories.

The new service center was decked out with at least a hundred floral wreaths and displays sent in by friends, customers, and suppliers. Within 10 minutes of the crowd's arrival, there wasn't a single bloom to be seen. Bouquets and instant corsages everywhere—but it made people happy and that was what was important. It took a crew of four strong men to get me from my office to the spot where the TV show would open. The shindig tied up streetcars and busses. Traffic was at a standstill. And things stayed that way until the mayor cut the blue ribbon and opened the center's doors. At 9:30 PM sharp, the show went on the air—and the open house was over—but the public lingered for several hours. This was our big day. And nobody had ever seen anything like it.

TELL IT LIKE IT IS

"Credibility Makes the Most Incredible Marketing"

I said it earlier: Advertising cannot be a gimmick. It must be believable and frank. It must resolve more questions for the customer than it raises. Straight and simple: THIS IS WHAT YOU GET. People overall haven't changed. The basic way to advertise cars really hasn't changed. But the media and the technology have changed. Television, for example, is so much more polished and technologically advanced today. A great tool, it can also get in the way of the information.

Remember the "OH WHAT A FEELING" Toyota ads that featured an effect called "the Toyota jump"? At the end of the pitch, the announcer was freeze-framed jumping in mid-air. That little twist was imitated far and wide all over the advertising and entertainment industries. An unforgettable achievement, but such campaigns are few and far between. Mostly, an ad has to do a job, and that job is to put a clear message across. Good lively music and snappy videos are fine, but forget the dancing girls and artsy-craftsy comedy.

Too often, the story line drowns out the message. Years ago, we shot a commercial in West Palm Beach at the Grapefruit League ballpark where the Expos and Braves train. The commercial had a baseball tie-in, but the spot was overrun with sports references. The pitcher may have been "throwing you a good deal," but you missed the deal because the baseball message was coming on so large and loud. The ad didn't get the marketing message across. When I screened it, I said: "I think I'm seeing a baseball game. What are we selling? Baseballs or cars?" We redid the ad and put the emphasis back on the product and the promotion.

Recently we shot a commercial on a lease payment program in which the lease payment included many features such as automatic transmission, air conditioning, AM-FM stereo. When I saw the review copy, I pointed out that those features were really important and needed more profile, more than one mention. Anybody can advertise a low payment, but not deliver all these extras in the car price. We re-edited the spot to emphasize *what* was included through both words and pictures. Every word in a 29.5-second-long ad must sell. You can't waste one. Get rid of phrases like "See your nearby dealer today!" For decades, those words seemed absolutely necessary, but what do they say that is new? "Come in now for this $179 lease!" tells you why you have to act and act now. That's what works: a direct, specific, and urgent call to action. Likewise, in television ads, every picture must count. Don't waste footage on less than the car's best angle...or a second or third favorite color.

As in everything else, marketing begins with people. The best marketing people, I think, are *not* the ones who try to dream up totally new ideas. Instead, they're sharp...but down-to-earth. They know how to borrow and massage an idea. They don't reinvent the wheel, but they can customize one and polish it up. A marketing person has to "look outward"—studying competitors and other industries, reading a lot, and watching trends, constantly looking for an "angle". At the heart of any great ad campaign, there is one word or one sentence or thought that captures it all. Even when I was doing TV ads back in Chicago, I would struggle to find that one word or sentence that would fit the product, the season, or the situation and then everything would fall into place.

Everybody thinks of marketing and advertising as glamorous and flashy. But, the most important work really happens behind the scenes. Will there be enough cars...and will they be in the right places? Are the incentives going to rally the sales force? Are we revving up our own people to be as excited and enthusiastic as the ads? When we launched the new Camry not long ago, we wanted the cars delivered to all of our dealers in one night. We set up a fireworks display at our Jacksonville Distribution Center just as the trucks took off to build excitement inside the company. We decided to let the folks in the Center know they were as much a part of the event as the ads or the salespeople in the stores.

What's the biggest mistake that I see made by advertisers? *Failing to put local advertising on top of a national blitz.* It's so easy to cut back local advertising when a national campaign for your product is going on. But national ads promote a product—not the local outlet. In our business, the Number One local advertiser is always the Number One dealer in sales and profits. If a dealer doesn't advertise, no one knows who you are, where you are, what you have for sale, or how you are better than your competition. Stop advertising and you might as well turn off your sign, shut off your lights, and lock the door. Why bother? You have just torn up your invitation to the customer.

The physical buildings of the Courtesy dealership were a very important part of my plan—both for their marketing potential and the role that they played in customer service. Even when I've operated sprawling buildings, I always focused on what the structure could *do*. After World War II, it was funny how many dealers would build huge mausoleums with a certain ethnic style to them. If they were Italian, the stores would have a Latin or Roman look. A French dealer would accent his building with Gothic charm. It was a way of telling the people in their old neighborhoods that the dealer had "arrived." To me, a dealership had to be workable, to move traffic through effectively, and to be easy to maintain and clean. The size of the columns or the beauty of the marble didn't matter.

My first major marketing move with Courtesy Ford was to strengthen the advertising power of the Courtesy building through signage and lighting. White Way Sign Company was an important factor in this promotion. Not only was White Way the number-one sign company in town, for some reason they got clearance to hang signs over sidewalks where no one else could win a permit to do so. Tom Flannery was White Way's owner, and he and I got along very well.

The tops of the buildings on both sides of Grand Avenue were leveled off to make them a common height, and the building exteriors were covered with white porcelain (just as gas stations of the time often were). Then sequentially flashing lights—called chasers—were installed around the tops of the buildings, that had the appearance of going around the whole block of structures on both sides of the street, two blocks long.

Tom salvaged the Ford sign that had just been taken down from the top of the Illinois Central Railroad building on Michigan Avenue. The sign had stood way up in the air, maybe 20 stories high. The F-O-R-D letters themselves were 10 feet tall. White Way rebuilt them and mounted them on top of our one-story building facing out to the street. Coming in at O'Hare airport to land one night, I looked down from a plane—the blaze of light from our dealership looked like a glistening *caravanserai* in a pitch black desert.

Above the front door on the northwest corner of the building was a lighted sign that proclaimed "The World's Largest Car Dealer." As the real icing on the cake, Tom Flannery built us a sign bigger than any theater sign in New York. We had to reinforce the entire building structure with steel beams running through the showroom and the roof to support it. It was 75–100 feet tall. On the top, it said, "Courtesy Ford". Those letters were five to six feet tall. The sign was double-faced and included a picture of the globe and my picture with me tipping my hat, all operated by a motor. Hal Barkun thought that up. I'm almost embarrassed to say that it became a major community landmark. The first day we turned it on, it blew all the lights in the neighborhood. A slew of unhappy neighbors showed up the next day. We listened and tried to explain, but it was after all, the power company's fault. The utility had underestimated the load and quickly put in a new panel and switchboard.

While we played it straight with our advertising, that didn't stop us from trying special events on the side that would spark attention for us. When the Thunderbird came out in 1955, we wanted to drop one from a helicopter onto a barge in Lake Michigan by the Wrigley Building. We couldn't buy adequate insurance to do it. Instead I got into a T-Bird convertible and all the salesmen followed me in other cars. We rolled down Michigan Avenue with our horns honking and staged an informal parade. (We actually applied for an official parade permit but were unable to get one.) Half of the office workers in the Loop must have waved and yelled "HI JIM!" to me that day.

In a restaurant on Michigan Avenue, we had house movers place a T-Bird on its side and then roll it through the main entrance into the restaurant's plate-glass show window display, placing our sign next to it. From the scratching of heads, we baffled almost every passerby as to how we were able to move that car into the restaurant. In addition to the showmanship T-Bird antics, we also did more conservative promotions such as placing pickup trucks in department stores where they were used as merchandise "dumps" for huge displays of candy or toys. These were at the time new marketing angles that certainly grabbed people's attention.

We became a favorite tour point for good-will visits to the United States. In 1959, the Soviet wrestling team stopped in. We had a mechanic nicknamed "Bolo", who was Polish and whose full name was Boleslawski. Bolo, a muscular fellow with strapping broad shoulders, had worked as a mechanic in a Russian prisoner-of-war camp during World War II and understood Russian fluently. When asked if he was a good mechanic, he would answer: "If not, I'd be dead!" When the Russians were coming, Bolo arrived at work in a business suit and didn't say one word. He stood on the showroom floor and listened, quietly telling us what our visitors said. The wrestling team members tried to get Ford technical manuals from us to take back with them, but we gave them brochures instead. They were fascinated by the Flip-Tops. In a corner of the used car department, we had an old SKODA, made in Czechoslovakia. Even new, this car was a flop. I think that our visitors were embarrassed by this souvenir of Communism.

The year 1959 was important to me for another reason—a personal one at the outset—but it later had an impact on our business promotions. When I turned 41 in 1959, I first became an avid swimmer. As a kid, swimming was a luxury. Lake Michigan was too far away and usually too cold. The Wilson Avenue YMCA, the closest pool, required a membership and charged a ten-cent soap-and-towel fee, which was out of the question for me. So I never really gave swimming much thought until later in life.

Handball, especially handball in an enclosed court, was a sport I grew to like in my twenties and thirties. During the late 1950s, I had gotten pretty good at the game and one opponent I particularly liked to match up against was Johnny

Bear—Chicago's athletic commissioner and a founder of the famous "Flying Bears" trapeze act.[11] During an intense game with me, Johnny suffered a heart attack. Despite everything all of us tried to do to revive him, it wasn't to be. Johnny's death made an impression on me, but I regarded it as a quirk. Three weeks later, though, another friend of mine—a priest named Father Cardinal—suffered the same fate in a handball match.

Out of the blue, my wife said to me, "Why don't you take up a less stressful competitive sport like swimming?" So, I did. My first day in the water, I could barely paddle across the pool's thirty-foot width. Steadily, however, I improved my conditioning and finally regularly stroked *sixty* sixty-foot lengths a day. I learned that swimming was a great conditioning and stretching exercise and an outstanding low-impact workout to build staying power. In fact, doing laps is when some of my very best business ideas occur to me. For me, it's a competitive sport; and the opponent is my own record of the previous day. Endurance swimming became and remains a keen interest of mine.

During my visits to Florida (which I'll describe later), a lifeguard from Grand Rapids, Michigan, named Joe Griffin would be swimming back and forth time and again off Hollywood Beach. He had tremendous endurance. I had always been interested in swimming, and we started talking. He told me that his life's dream was to swim from Chicago to Michigan City—36.75 miles—no easy feat because the water of Lake Michigan is rough and cold. After a while, we decided to sponsor him and provide him with guide boats. Although he didn't make it, the event stirred up a tremendous amount of publicity. When he tried again the next year, we saw the publicity potential for our business.

---

[11]Clayton "Lone Ranger" Moore was also a member of the "Flying Bears" during the early years of his career. Clayton grew up about three blocks away from me. He is about ten years older than I am...and, yes, I do remember what he looked like before he became a masked man.

We would follow him all night long and send out bulletins to the press as to where Joe was. The Chicago disk jockey Howard Miller even did remote radio broadcasts from the guide boat. Then we turned the swims into a contest, and the big prize became $10,000 and then later $25,000. The swim took in nearly all of our regional selling area. Then we opened it up to a long swim across Lake Michigan from Chicago to Benton Harbor.

Abdel-Latif Abo-Heif was a major in the United Arab Republic Army stationed in Alexandria, Egypt, and he trained by swimming up and down the Nile. I never saw another competitive swimmer with his drive and stamina. He would start out at a pace of a mile every 20 minutes. Two or three might keep up for the first five miles. Then they would drop back. The UAR major never let up, completed the swim, and won the $25,000 and returned to Egypt. His wife was an opera singer. I asked him what he would do with the money. His dream was to buy a villa, staff it with servants, and retire on the banks of the Nile. I never heard from him again, but he became a celebrity on Egyptian television for his feat.

Special events that would create excitement were always on our minds—especially ones that would please children. We bought an old "American La France" fire engine pumper. It came with a complete record of where it had been used over many decades. With seats installed in the back, we took the children for a ride around the block after school and on weekends; but I'm not sure the neighbors appreciated the noise. The fire engine was *not* a TV success. The first time that the engine's brightly lit, brilliant red finish connected with the gaze of old-time, glare-sensitive television, it blew up the camera!

One day, a little old man came by with a "pony" cart with a surrey top that seated about eight kids and was pulled by a team of two small horses. We couldn't do without an attraction like this, I thought to myself. Many people travelled a long way to bring their kids in for rides after we presented the cart on TV. That also went around the block, the same as the fire engine—spring through fall.

Our poor neighbors. We were the magnet for lots of traffic. People would park as far as two blocks away. The neighbors couldn't get out of their driveways sometimes. Customers would block our neighbors' driveways when they parked, or the customers would take spots in front of fire-plugs. In the fall, the holidays brought new events. Starting Thanksgiving week, the dealership was spruced up for Christmas with a Wurlitzer juke box—booming out "Jingle Bells" and "Joy to the World" and all the other favorites con-tinuously at 500 watts. That on top of the pony rides and the fire engine. Thinking back about it, we should have been more considerate of our neighbors' right to quiet and priva-cy. No doubt, that's why automobile dealers are today zoned into auto rows in most cities…and you can certainly follow the reasoning.

One special attraction that the neighbors never mind-ed was the quietest one that we ever offered. We hired a man who would stand at one spot in the showroom and never smile or move a muscle, as hard as the kids would try to tease him.

Then there was Santa. Each year a Santa Claus would give toys to all the children. In those days, you could buy what seemed like all the toys in the world for $10,000. Truckloads would come from Japan and Taiwan. We even had little transistor radios, which were still a big novelty back in the late fifties. Maybe they received only two stations, but they played. (Little did I suspect back then that today we would be regularly signing checks with ten digits *before* the decimal point for Japanese merchandise and that it would be the highest quality in the world.)

Santa Claus at Christmas time was fun. But our televi-sion presence allowed us to do some serious Santa Claus work for charity year-round. Starting back in the Hudson days, we staged telethons for the Heart Fund, Cancer Soci-ety, Cerebral Palsy and a host of other charities. Perhaps the biggest telethon campaign was for the City of Hope where the contributors built a wing for leukemia patients. After I had done some major charity campaigning for several years in a row, Irv Kupcinet put an appeal in his column: "Isn't there anyone in Chicago willing to take some of this on and give Jim Moran a rest?" I appreciated that.

We had a parade of stars of the time join us for these fund-raisers: Bob Hope, Eydie Gorme, George Jessel, Jack Carson, the Cisco Kid and Pancho, Mickey Rooney, Buddy Ebsen, Don McNeill, Raymond Burr, Melvyn Douglas, Mayor Daley—the list went on and on. We would donate our own TV time, and there was always a certain adrenaline rush that would keep all of us involved going through the entire event. Fortunately, doing 60 laps a day at the Illinois Athletic Club pool gave me good stamina. A lot of money was raised for worthy causes through this use of television, and it's one part of television that I miss even to this day.

With all of the big, national-scale drives that we undertook, two very local appeals stick out in my memory. Bob Boyd was a Ford dealer on the south side of Chicago. He had been stricken with an inoperable heart condition and was undergoing hospitalization at St. Mary's. His dealership was not exactly a big one. Instead of doing our regular Friday night commercials during the breaks, I said instead that Courtesy Motors would obviously like to sell everyone a new car, but we can't. If it's too far for you to drive, why don't you stop by and visit Bob Boyd's Ford store on the South Side. When Bob made it out of the hospital, he stopped by and told me that I would be the first one to get his store when he left the business. I declined his offer; but the episode stuck with me, that just a mention like that could have meant so much.

A much larger-scale tragedy touched the heart of all Chicago. On Monday, December 1, 1958, a fire swept through the Our Lady of the Angels Catholic School. It was a nightmare. More than 90 children were killed, as were three nuns.[h] Countless others were burned and maimed. Trapped kids were jumping out of second-story windows

and missing the rescue nets because of the smoke and con-
fusion. That night we scrapped our ads on the TV show and
started a fund for the children and their families. By then, I
had been through a lot of telethons, but I don't ever remember raising money with more passion than on that
evening. I will never forget visiting the hospital that night afterwards and looking at the children. One little girl—whom
I remember vividly—was burned over 75 percent of her
body. The Courtesy Associates really came through, donat-
ing $3,000. The fund itself raised $40,000. The families and
the Church appreciated our efforts, but how can you ever
make up for a loss like that?

My wife and I—together with our children—regularly
attended church as a family. Although I was active in our
parish, was an usher at Sunday Mass, and made a contribution to the building of our new Basilica, the Church and I
didn't always see eye-to-eye. We started after-church open-
ings of the dealership in 1949, back in the Hudson days, but
they became a major political/religious issue during my second association with Ford. The restaurants, the movie houses, and the amusement parks would be open on Sunday.
People would look at new homes then. So, why not car dealerships? This was the second biggest purchase a family made.
Shopping for a car then was as much family recreation as
anything else. We wouldn't open before noon. On TV, we
would invite people to come on down after church and to
bring the kids. We have plenty for you to eat. Hot dogs and
hamburgers were the most popular fare. We let viewers
know that we had a place where we could entertain their
children while they shopped for a car.[12]

---

[12] I can remember in the early days when we were *closed* on Sundays. On one
Monday morning, we came to work and our safe was actually gone from the
showroom floor. The next day Brinks came in and cut a hole in the concrete
floor in the showroom about four feet by four feet; workers welded it to the
ground with steel struts, covering the supports with a foot of concrete. As
the years went on, a lot less business was done for cash, but I still always felt a
little safer being open on Sundays.

Even in the fifties, many Christians (and Catholics especially) were bound by religious or semi-religious convictions regarding shopping on Sunday. I always disagreed with that practice. Even my friends the parish priests would preach from the pulpit that it was sinful to work on Sunday, but after Mass, I would—more than once—see them out as guests enjoying a juicy cut of prime rib in a restaurant or playing golf. Well, what about the serving people and cooks working in those restaurants or the staff of the clubhouse? Sunday was really the only day that many families could get together and consider a major purchase like a house or a car.

All the dealers in Chicago banded together in about 1956 and did some arithmetic. Jim Moran is selling more than 300 new and used cars on a typical Sunday, they calculated. Given that fact, they decided that becoming a tad more religious was in *their* own best interest. "If you can't lick Moran on the selling floor, putting him out of business on his busiest day was the next best answer." My feeling was that no one person's or religion's day of worship should be singled out.

The dealers persuaded a judge to issue a Sunday closing declaration. It applied only to car dealerships but had nothing at all to say about saloons or even burlesque houses. I filed a 30-day injunction and took it to the Illinois Supreme Court, claiming conspiracy. "Why don't you close the movie theaters and shut down the saloons?" I asked. Seeing that the declaration was clearly unconstitutional, the Supreme Court backed our position 7–0, and the news made the front-page headlines in the *Chicago Tribune*.

Because of our prominence in the marketplace and because of our advertising, more and more, we became news. In Chicago, the words "Torture Time" were nearly synonymous with Courtesy Ford and with me. After a commercial break began and before I would start one of my messages, I would always warn the audience that "Torture Time" was about to start and that this might be the right moment to go to the kitchen and make a sandwich...or to adjourn to the bathroom to shower. Funny thing: people just generally stayed put. Maybe they wanted to know what they might be missing.

Paul Molloy, a columnist for the *Chicago Sun-Times*, wrote a piece about me taping 18 minutes of commercials within an hour and a quarter. Experts tell me that's working at a pretty fast pace. Molloy wrote, "No script. No direction. No temperament." Paul must have caught me on a good day. He *did* describe the time that I accidentally roped my legs to a bumper with a microphone cord and "pleaded into live cameras, 'Will somebody get me out?'"

One of Paul's comments about the taping sessions was especially perceptive:

"What's interesting about this is that Moran didn't do…commercials [with flaws] over, deciding to go with the bloopers. He wasn't just being humble; he was being canny, for mistakes are the mark of the ordinary guy, and ordinary guys like to buy Fords from ordinary guys—and enough ordinary guys last year gave him $41,000,000 worth of business." [i]

The goofs were never faked, but being natural truly brought me closer to the viewers and helped earned their trust.

More and more publicity came our way. In 1961, *Time* magazine wanted to do a story on Courtesy Motors, and I said, "No, thank you." I didn't want national publicity, concerned that some unbalanced person might harm my family. The magazine said that they were going to do a story whether I liked it or not and whether I cooperated or not. So we decided to cooperate. Hal Barkun helped me tremendously in preparing for the interviews.

No one, however, could have prepared me for what happened afterward. *Time* brought the famous photographer Alfred Eisenstaedt—who died a few months ago at 96—in to take the pictures, and they called their report the "Heyday of the Haggle." An "article" became a "feature story." A "feature story" became THE COVER STORY.[j] As far as I know, I'm the only car dealer ever to have appeared on the cover of *Time*. The article portrayed me as a cross between

Gunsmoke's Marshal Matt Dillon, Liberace, and Bishop Fulton Sheen. Whomever they were talking about was not the same guy that I met in the mirror every morning.

Things were never quite the same again. Letters poured in from all over the world. People started backing me for mayor. The networks sent out feelers to see if I wanted to do national TV. You have to remember, TV stars such as George Burns and Arthur Godfrey were as much salespeople as entertainment personalities. Harry Truman sold men's clothing. Betty Furness—The Westinghouse Lady—went on to become a consumer affairs official both nationally and locally in New York. And Ronald Reagan was a television pitchman for both Twenty Mule Team Borax and General Electric for years. But I had a hard time taking all this about politics or national television very seriously. I was a car dealer and happy being one.

The possibility of a visible role in the world of baseball presented the only really serious temptation to be more than a car dealer. I had heard that the chewing-gum baron Philip Wrigley wanted to sell the Chicago Cubs and Wrigley Field. I went to Frank Schreiber who was President and General Manager of WGN-TV, along with Hal Barkun. "Frank, if Philip Wrigley is serious about selling Wrigley Field and the team, I'd like to see if we could negotiate a sale to me." Then Frank said kiddingly that I could of course *give* them the television rights.

In any case, the first talks went forward. My friends at WGN didn't have far to walk to set up the meeting. The Wrigley Building is right across from the Tribune Tower. When I walked into Mr. Wrigley's office, I can still recall the huge bowl chock full of Juicy Fruit, Doublemint, and Wrigley's Spearmint sticks on his secretary's desk. The offices were large but not pretentious.

"No introduction is needed. I see you on television often. Please have a seat," was the way that *he* opened the conversation. After a while, it became clear that he thought that I was coming over to ask about giving packets of

Wrigley gum away at Courtesy Motors. I told him that I really wanted to talk to him about the ball club and its potential sale. I said that I was interested. He did a double-take and said, *"You are?"*

I said that if a fair price could be negotiated I'd like to buy the team and rent the stadium. Then he asked me to tell him a little bit about myself. He wanted to know where I lived now and earlier and if I had a college background. His face seemed to sag a little as I told him that my early social set was streetcar society and not the Chicago Yacht Club. He then told me that owning a baseball team requires a man of a certain social as well as business stature. He frankly didn't know if I'd be accepted but he said that he would think about it. "You don't have to call me. Mr. Jacobs will get in touch with you through Mr. Schreiber." I knew what the answer was right then, although Frank called me a couple of days later and confirmed that "social stature" was going to be the stumbling block.

The *Time* magazine circuit itself was pretty heady. Shortly after the article appeared in March of 1961, *Time* staged an event at the Waldorf Astoria in Manhattan. They invited every individual on whom they had done a cover story. The *Time* event at the Waldorf was quite an affair. All the Kennedys were there—Jack, Bobby, and Teddy. I remember running into Bobby and Teddy in the lobby. I had met them before in Chicago at Eunice Kennedy Shriver's house. They were both so very young. Bobby still was Attorney General at the time. I told Bobby that his New England accent sounded more like Jack Kennedy than Jack sounded like himself. The Waldorf gathering was followed by a second event. Once a year, *Time* calls in all of their correspondents from around the world. This time they got together in Bermuda. They asked me to come down to address their people. They put me on the agenda right after Henry Luce, *Time's* founder.

After appearing on the cover of *Time* and—independent of that—Courtesy Ford was probably reaching the high-point of its success, Ford Motor Company sent their regional manager in to see me. He said that my TV shows were so powerful that the other dealers in the area didn't have an equal opportunity competing in the marketplace. *"Of course they do,"* was my answer. He persisted, claiming that Courtesy Ford was unique and I had a way of ingratiating myself to people and earning their confidence. His closing message was that Ford would build four huge dealerships just on the outskirts of Chicago within seven to eight miles of Courtesy. His visit occurred in 1964 and the economy then was pretty strong.

Ford was going to completely fund putting aggressive dealers in these locations, he said. It sounded to me like they wanted to put me out of business and I told him so. (It was a lot like an earlier discussion that I had with Ford in 1946.) No, no, he said and told me they would offer me a Lincoln-Mercury or Ford dealership anywhere I wanted to go, but nothing within 500 miles of Chicago.

Ford went on to build the gorgeous new dealerships. Even then, I could see the strong growth trend toward the suburbs. The legitimate expansion around Chicago was going to give Ford a very plausible reason for changing how Fords would be sold in the metropolitan area and changing who would be selling them. As baseball manager Casey Stengel used to say: "You gotta lose 'em sometime. When you do, lose 'em right." [k]

When I look back at the Chicago era, what *really* sticks in my memory?

I guess the zany things most of all. Our monthly steak-and-beans meetings, at which our best sales performers would feast on juicy porterhouse and Idaho potatoes...and the not-so-lucky made do with pork-and-beans.

The snow. How can I ever forget the snow? I can remember one year when it cost $45,000 just to get rid of the snow. And, even with the outside help, our whole staff was decked out in galoshes and gloves...and armed with brooms to brush off the cars outside. After one blizzard, we staged a

"June in January" sales event and worked for two days in the middle of January to clean the streets and the lot of all the snow, while most of the streets were declared to be in a snow emergency. I still remember my TV commercial verbatim, "We know your cars are snowbound. If you come down, we'll trust that you'll describe your present car's trade-in value honestly." It worked. People were fair, and we were the only dealer selling cars.

I can remember the November that Ford called and asked if we could take a fleet of 500 convertibles, built in their San Jose plant. I thought back about some fun times in my 1932 PB Plymouth, and I said: "Let's do it." My sales manager and controller just about had heart attacks. When we featured the romance of the convertible on television, we sold them all—all 500 of them.

I could go on for pages more than anybody would want me to, I'm sure. Here are some of the choicest highlights:

In the earlier Hudson years, one customer traded his Chevy for a Hudson, then decided he wanted to trade back that Hudson for a Chevy similar to the one he had. This was after two years had gone by...and unwittingly we ended up selling his Chevy back to him. (The car had been traded in again by another customer.) After we cleared the misunderstanding up, it turned into quite an endorsement for our reconditioning work.

Another fellow tried to sell us a used car that he had repainted and modified a little. His case was a bit different since he had actually *stolen* the auto from us. We got the car back...and he was sentenced to a year in jail.

One night, as cars were queuing up for the TV spots, two onlookers wanted one of them so badly that they started a bidding war, tossing money into the back seat. We were able to calm them down before the commercial break and invited them back to the dealership to actually draw straws for the right to buy it.

Once we bought a Chrysler New Yorker, intended for Queen Elizabeth's coronation. It was going to be a crowd drawer. The car had been painted purple, and all the trim was gold plated. Even the upholstery and the special footrests had royal seals on them. We took this car on consignment and used it as a conversation piece on television, but once we did a trace on the car's papers, we learned that it was stolen—fortunately not from Her Highness but from a promoter. We of course returned it.

5

A Future in Florida

1966–1968

In 1951, I visited Florida for the first time. It was to take a vacation, and we stayed at the Hollywood Beach Hotel. This hotel had a stunning driveway and entranceway. The gorgeous landscaping featured an Olympic size pool on the grounds—measuring 100 feet by 40 feet. In addition, the hotel overlooked 1,000 feet of oceanfront. The dining room could easily seat 400 people and was presided over by a maitre d', named McGuire, who always dressed in a bright green suit. Whenever he wanted somebody's attention he would snap a rubber band against the menu in his hand. At each table, guests were served by a butter girl, a roll boy, and a personal waiter or waitress. A guest felt like royalty. The hotel's kitchen was excellent. The guests who could afford to stay at the Hollywood Beach Hotel surely had the money and the taste to go anywhere.

We would travel down to Florida on *The Floridian* out of Chicago's Union Station, back at a time when train travel was also a luxury. Train service like that is now a distant memory in the United States, and my favorite hotel closed its doors some years ago.

Visiting Florida for several weeks during each winter became a regular habit after 1953. Health problems that first afflicted my wife and then myself ultimately prompted us to move to Florida for good. My first wife—Arline—was becoming an invalid, afflicted with rheumatoid arthritis. The Florida climate agreed with her. Any little improvement meant a lot because she seemed to be (and ultimately was) destined to life in a wheelchair, just as her grandmother had been. I can still remember the day that she came home from the doctor with news about a new wonder drug that might change everything for her: cortisone. She was 27 at the time.

She took 150 mg of cortisone a day, and her arthritis seemed to disappear. But the dosage had to be increased steadily to have an impact. Nobody at the time realized how destructive that drug could be. Then we learned of the horrible side effects. Her adrenal glands virtually vanished, and her heart was hopelessly weakened. Because of the drug's menacing side effects, she ended up living out the final years of her life in the wheelchair she had hoped to avoid.

I always felt she fought courageously. She was a wonderful lady and a good person. Above all, she was the person who raised our children, and she did that with enviable devotion. Several times near the end of her life I asked her: "Maybe *we* should have done this differently?" Her answer was firm: "No, my grandmother died of arthritis in a wheelchair when she was 36. At least I lived to be 60 and had the chance to raise my family."

It was during one of my wife's hospitalizations, back in 1965 in Chicago, that I first learned that I had cancer. My wife was in the hospital because of cortisone side effects that led to hematomas if she bumped anything. From my mother's side, I had inherited a series of moles on my body. I had learned to be on the lookout for any change in their condition or appearance.

Despite my medical discharge from the Army, I had been in good "everyday" health. The heart condition would have been a risk in combat, but it was something that I learned to live with. I credit my stamina then to regular exercise, particularly swimming. To have such a seemingly inconsequential symptom as changes in two moles turn out to be rapidly spreading and almost certainly lethal melanoma was beyond my comprehension. The moles on my right arm had gone from brown to black. In fact I had gone to a dermatologist—who by then had been treating me for about a year—the week before, and he told me that if anything was really wrong he'd cut my arm off. That was the kind of radical surgery common back then. I only wish that his diagnosis was as thorough as his talk was confident.

My wife was under the care of a new physician, a young doctor by the name of George Panczyszyn. For most people, George's last name was a nightmare to remember, but I'll never forget the spelling. George saved my life.

He looked at the moles and asked me how long they had been in that condition. I explained that I had been seeing a doctor for about a year. George also asked another doctor in the hall. They both said that the moles looked like trouble. Even though the next day was Sunday, George told me to meet him in the emergency room and to have the moles cut out. If it was nothing, the result would just be a few stitches. In I went at 8 AM. After he took the growths out, he went up to the pathology lab and learned that these moles had turned malignant. It was melanoma. "What do we do now?" I asked. He told me to report back the next day for radical surgery. The cancer was so near my lymph glands in the neck and shoulders that it might have already attacked the gland system.

When I first learned that I had cancer, I felt my whole world come crashing down. George explained that the operation could take an hour or maybe five hours. I was scared but I tried to be realistic. "George, you're the doctor. Do whatever it takes." After five and a half hours, I was wheeled out of surgery looking like a mummy. You can still put a fist under my arm in the cavity where everything was cut out. They did a radical removal of lymph nodes from my armpit.[13] When my family came in to see me, I had more tubes and drains running out of me than you could count. Trying to bolster my spirits, my kids joked around with me that I looked like a potato that had sprouted "eyes."

Privately Doctor Panczyszyn told me that the cancer had penetrated my lymph glands and that my chances of survival and recovery were about 10 percent. "Now we wait," he said. "Do we pray?" I asked. "No, we hope that you are on the right side of the numbers," the good doctor answered. I stayed in the hospital for 14 days as they made skin grafts and disengaged the tubing. Doctors had stripped the main artery in my arm and then reattached it.

One month after the dressings were gone, I went back to running Courtesy, but then I had a recurrence six months later. That bumped my odds down to five percent. Doctor Panczyszyn said that it looked like the cancer was now in the bloodstream and that it would probably spread throughout my body. I had somewhere between six months and three years left. It was going to be a painful and unpleasant death. I went home and told my wife.

If I hadn't been afflicted with cancer and told that I had only a short time to live, I certainly wouldn't have made the move to Florida as early as I did. But the "death sentence" made up my mind. I loved the sand and sun, and I had shoveled enough snow and been bundled up in enough scarves to last me a lifetime. Ford's suburban strategy also meant that I was going to be up against an all out competitive fight with other Ford dealers. Would it be worth it? I decided to sell

---

[13] Over the years, I've become cooler under fire, as I've faced major medical ordeals. On the night before I had my open-heart surgery in May 1988, the medical staff came in and ran down what was going to happen. I listened and they explained everything exceptionally well, but I had only one question of the chief surgeon when they were all done with their briefing, and that was: "How long before I can go home?"

Courtesy Ford to my former son-in-law Tom Beddia and the general sales manager, Dick Benedetto, as equal partners and to move to Florida to die.[14]

There was an oceanfront home in Hillsboro that hadn't sold for two years because it only had two bedrooms. But, the lot was great, with ocean frontage and the Intracoastal Waterway behind the property. The Waterway gave me a place where I could dock my boat. I made the owners the ridiculous offer of $150,000. They accepted it. Inside of 60 days, I had moved to Florida, and the calendar had flipped over to 1967.

It was almost exactly a mile from my home to the lighthouse, the egress to the ocean, called the Hillsboro Inlet. I swam there every day and would walk or jog back. I'd have my days when I thought that I would lick the disease. On others not. Everybody with cancer whom I have known wavers between resignation and fighting it, mostly in the latter case to keep up the spirits of their loved ones. Overall, you pretty well accept the fact that school might be out.

Waiting for a major worsening in my health, my condition ironically seemed to stabilize, and I was regaining my old strength and stamina. Then Doctor Panczyszyn, to whom I was very grateful, said that he wouldn't mind coming down to Florida himself with his wife and family. His two boys were ages nine and eleven. At first he wanted to try Florida life for a month. If it were to work out, he asked for help in finding an entry-level position on the staff of Holy Cross Hospital. I told him that I would welcome him being in Florida to look after Arline, keep her medication in balance...and watch out for my condition too.

---

[14] Officially, I turned over the keys to Courtesy on New Year's Eve 1967. The Courtesy facilities were ultimately leveled. Today the land is the site of a big Jewel grocery center and an Osco Drugstore—Osco is a division of Jewel. The Jewel is on one side, and the Osco and parking are on the other. It's my understanding that these went on to become the biggest volume locations in these chains.

I said that I wanted to get him a condo about 500 feet from ours, but the doctor felt that it would be too expensive and that he couldn't afford it. I went ahead, bought and furnished it. I told him not to worry about being able to afford it. "Prices are increasing," I told him. "Pay me when you have a chance."

One day, during his initial visit, George confided that he didn't know how to swim. I asked to teach him. He was only 41 but a big fellow—over six feet tall and weighing a hefty 230 pounds. It wasn't easy. George could only stay afloat in the pool with the help of huge rubber flipper fins. Unless he wore them, he would sink like a brick.

Just before the end of the 30-day stay, his kids were in the ocean on a rubber raft, out about 50 to 75 feet from shore. It was lunch time. George called them to come in. They ignored him. His wife Mary told him to calm down and not to let his temper get the better of him. He called a third time, and they still didn't come back. They were very young at the time and did not realize the danger to their father. He ran down the five flights of stairs straight into the ocean, still wearing his shoes, and plunged into the ocean at high tide. Three minutes later he was dead. It was the very day that he had taken and passed his board exams for licensing in Florida.

Although all of this was happening nearly next door to me, I was completely unaware of it until George's wife Mary telephoned. Her voice was horror-struck, "Jim, come over. George is dead. He's drowned." I hopped in the car—out of instinct, I would have to say—and was there in a minute. The local police were still giving him artificial respiration, but it was hopeless. I had lost a good friend, and medicine was robbed of a brilliant physician. It wasn't very much to do after such a loss but we were at least able to sell the condo, and this money bought a home for the family who wanted to leave the condo and return to Chicago—too many bad memories. My wife's deteriorating health, my bout with cancer, and George's death—all put me in touch with my own mortality and how very fragile life was.

After a year of swimming to the Lighthouse and jogging back, I was tiring of the routine and itching for a new challenge. My life had been cars, and I was anxious to be back in the business. After my unhappy episodes with Ford, I had no interest in another Ford dealership; especially since I had helped to get the Chevy-to-Ford new car sales ratio in Chicago from 4:1 down to 2:1, and Ford showed their appreciation by surrounding me with four new factory dealerships. Chrysler was no alternative. Chrysler headquarters in Highland Park wrestled with serious quality problems with their cars during the sixties. Having to handle the Chrysler products of that time would have been shades of my old Hudson days. General Motors seemed to be the way to go. From a respect that had begun with my early fascination with Buicks, I had long wanted a General Motors dealership; this seemed to be the right time to do something about it.

By the middle sixties, the real dynamo in the General Motors lineup was Pontiac.[15] Pontiac was as hot then as Toyota is today. Bunky Knudsen, John De Lorean, and Pete Estes were Pontiac's top team; and they were in their prime. Knudsen defined Pontiac's new mindset when he said that *you can sell an old man a young man's car, but you can't sell a young man an old man's car*. Knudsen and his colleagues were bound and determined to make Pontiac a *young man's car*. Pontiac became renowned for their sporty performance vehicles, and the rejuvenated nameplate ignited the stock-car circuit with drivers like "Fireball" Roberts.

Everybody (especially Yankee "snowbird" dealers such as myself who had fled the winters in the north) wanted a sunbelt Pontiac franchise, but there were none to be had. There were no open available dealership locations in all of Florida, except for a very modest site in Homestead. The

---

[15] While the Pontiac was a great American car for its time, even the very best American cars were still dealing with some important quality challenges that weren't to be truly mastered until the later 1980s.

owner operated a gas station, retailed between 12 to 15 new Pontiacs a month, and was considering selling out. At the time, Homestead was little more than a village of vegetable and fruit farms (snap beans and little red potatoes were the local specialties) snuggled up against the Homestead Air Force Base. The town only had 2,500 people and, of course, your occasional 'gator or snake. I-95 and the turnpike were still on the drawing boards. The drive to and from my home to the site would be an hour and 45 minutes each way on A1A.

Added to the inconvenience, small local market size, and meager facilities, General Motors also set up a real obstacle course for me to secure a dealership at all. Before General Motors would agree to give me the franchise, they checked me backwards and forwards. I had to give my word to the Vice President of the Pontiac Division that I would personally not go on television. Local Pontiac management was deathly afraid that I would become a television celebrity and pull customers from all over Dade and Broward counties. Your word is your bond, as my mother said. I had to say OK. It was a little easier to do since I really didn't want to return to the stressful life of being a high-visibility TV spokesman again anyway. I signed the papers in 1968 and was back in the auto business.

"Jim Moran's leadership and grasp of the local marketplace combined with his relentless commitment to innovation are what have allowed his team to set the pace in auto retailing time and again. That's as true today as it was decades ago."

— *Dick Knox*
Retired Senior Vice President,
Development Division
JM Family

The dealership sat directly next to the railroad tracks. For $75 a month, I rented the one little office building, a concrete platform, a wooden shed with 4x4's (as a drive-in), and a one-car garage with a roll-up door where the parts were kept locked up with a padlock. The only phone sat on the bookkeeper's desk with an extension of the same line in the parts department. The service department was outdoors, and a vinyl sheet covered the car wash. I had no office, there was really no showroom, and customers could barely find the place. Still, Homestead kept me occupied; and at least I was back in the car business, being able to take on the sales objective of building sales from 12 to 15 cars a month...to 40 or 50. If anything, this was going to be a challenge and something I really wanted to do.

I had the intention of building a new facility in Homestead immediately. It was about then that I first met Dick Knox, who was Pontiac's parts-and-services manager for the zone. He came to me with some architectural suggestions from the home office for the new Homestead dealership that I was going to build. The data that he brought said Homestead had the market potential for 25 cars a month. I took his architectural plans into my kitchen and looked at Dick in a puzzled way, "These look pretty good, but where am I going to put my miniature railroad track? You know I'm going to sell 160 cars a month. When families drive down all the way from Miami, the kids have to have something to do. And what about the car wash...and the hot dog stand, where will they go?" He was a little taken aback.

"A dealer who had been with an American automobile manufacturer once told me that, because of Jim Moran's expertise, he learned more in working with Jim Moran over five years than working with Detroit over twenty-five years."

—John Williams
Executive Vice President,
JM Family and General Manager
SET

TELL IT LIKE IT IS

"The Art of the Dealership"

Do you want to run a successful dealership? Then you have to follow three commandments. The first commandment is "Be there". The second commandment is "Be there" and the third is—you guessed it—"Be there", too.

Dealers should be on the job every day. Control and discipline are part of the reason—yes—but the biggest need is to provide leadership and to build enthusiasm among the staff. An on-the-ball dealership buzzes with activity. Since most of the business comes in the evening and on weekends, a dealership really has to hum at a time when most "professional managers" are polishing their putts or stretching out on a Barcalounger.

Every day—but not always at the *same* time—good dealers walk their dealerships in their entirety, and *they look at it as if they were customers.* Is it neat, clean, attractive...front to back? *In a dealership, housekeeping is worth money.* Is the waiting room nice enough to sit in for several hours? And, how about the cleanliness of the restrooms? Are the technicians' stalls, lifts, and work benches cleaned every night...or are they caking up with grease and dirt?

Customers relate the cleanliness and neatness of a store to the quality and reliability of the cars sold there. How confident do you feel when you climb aboard a dirty airliner? How confident would you be about buying a car from a dealership with skid-row looks? The inside and outside of a showroom are as important to a dealership as personal appearance is to a human being. The showroom should be a jewel box with windows cleaned, floors glistening or cleanly carpeted—all whetting the customer's appetite to buy NOW. Pair that with confident, friendly treatment and how can you lose?

Top-notch dealers will walk through their parts area, aisle-by-aisle, with their eyes taking in every bin and especially the tops of the bins. Have the bins been vacuumed recently? Are there parts piled on the floor, on top of the bins, or off to the side in a corner? Is the whole area so clean and well organized that you would want to bring a customer back to see it? The retail parts display for service customers who are waiting should look every bit as inviting to browse as the accessory area in an auto specialty store. Is it just so-so, or does it really sparkle with items that people will want to buy? *For a dealer, the next worst thing to not putting cars out on the road is putting cars out there without the proper service and parts backup.* A good dealer shows up at 7:00 AM more than a few mornings each month and sees how service customers are greeted and treated, especially how their complaints are handled. (A dealer knows that his or her personally listening to as many complaints as possible helps cut their number.) Good service is like a dream come true. But, service satisfaction has to be *real*. Listen to customers and satisfy their complaints, and it will boost a dealer's reputation and new car sales like nothing else. Technicians should be rewarded for no "come backs"; for doing it right the first time. Money, recognition and real involvement will tell "techs" how important they are to the customer and to the success of the dealership.

There are no big secrets in the used car business. A dealership that is well stocked with properly conditioned used cars, and that upholds a good reputation, should always be the most successful and profitable dealer selling *new* cars. Almost always, a successful dealer maintains an even balance between new and used car sales. The big key to selling used cars is to "turn" them quickly. After they're taken in trade, they should be gone in 45 days—*max*.

Is there a good mix of used cars on the lot—so you can serve customers with a whole range of vehicles—and are the best ones front line? Are all the cars "detailed"—carefully cleaned and in trim shape inside and out? On the inspection tour, does the dealer open and check trunks, glove boxes, and engine compartments? In the used car division, how are the closing offices? Clean, nice, comfortable chairs? Or, don't customers even want to sit down?! Take a good close look. Some of them I have been in, I couldn't wait to get out of.

Car retailing is a different business today. As the customer demand for services has risen, finance and insurance have become a very important part of what a dealer offers. To serve the customer and the dealer well in these businesses—good dealers know—demands special training. What hasn't changed is: *Building loyalty and goodwill is the heart of the dealership.*

Once I was in business again, I quickly had volume and expansion on my mind. We had been operating Homestead for about six months and had increased Pontiac sales about 300 percent. From the very beginning, I knew that I would have to build another store in Homestead and I acquired property on Federal Highway. After I started building the new Homestead store, a dealership point opened in Hollywood, Florida, and this looked like a great location. Luck was with me. I was given the Hollywood dealership.

After General Motors' initial reluctance to give me a Florida dealership at all, what made them willing to grant me the great franchise in Hollywood? First, I had begun to know some of the Pontiac management team such as Al Hendrickson and Dick Knox and had shown them the depth of my marketing conviction. Second, south Florida was the largest daily rental-car market in the United States, but Pontiac had a weak presence in the local rental business. I had the reputation of knowing the fleet rental sales business from my Chicago days. When we got the Hollywood site, I had to sell the Homestead location before it opened, and the stipulation against my appearing on television continued.

Hollywood would also be a totally new facility, so we had some elbow room as to where we would locate. My original plan was to be further east, closer to the ocean, but an elderly real estate expert persuaded my Chicago business associate Herb Tousley and myself that we wanted to be farther west. The property that has since become Hollywood Lincoln-Mercury, at Highway One and Sheridan, was for sale. The owners wanted $800,000, which was too rich for my blood at the time. When we went to the bank for a loan, the bank wanted more collateral than just the property itself. So we passed and looked farther west.

I first met Herb Tousley when I was a Hudson dealer and Herb was an executive vice president for a finance company, called Universal Commercial Investment Trust. I used Herb's company to floorplan our automobiles and to finance installment purchases for customers.[16] Herb grew up poor, left the Emerson school in Minneapolis with a sixth-grade education and went to work driving a horse-and-wagon. He supported his mother from the time he turned 15. Then he earned his driver's license and drove trucks until he was 23. He was big, strong, and tough. By 23, he wanted to do anything but drive a truck, so he took a job as a collector for a finance company for $150 a month. He remained with the same firm until he was 60, advancing to a vice presidency and spending his free time hunting bear and fishing for trout in the mountains of Montana. In 1968, he joined me in Florida.

Herb's friend—the real estate expert—was right about where we should build our new dealership. Sheridan Street and U.S. 441—the ultimate site of my Pontiac dealership— are today in the heart of Hollywood. When we acquired the Hollywood property, I still remember a sign across the street offering land for $40 an acre. Today you couldn't buy a patch of land big enough to hold a tiny sign for $40! The Hollywood location was a mixed forest including fruit trees, and there were a fair number of farmers who grew mangoes nearby. There was a lot of junk in the wooded area that had been deposited there over the years by a heavy construction firm that had access to the land.

Another person who was enormously important to me was Marilyn Boesken. Marilyn began working as my administrative assistant in May 1969. She started the day after she interviewed and stayed for nearly 25 wonderful years. Loyalty incarnate and quick on the uptake! All I had to do was to have a certain look, and she knew what had to be done. When a stroke blinded my right eye in 1984 and I

---

[16]After cars are shipped to a dealer, somebody must pay for them and that's what the finance company did. When we sold them, then we paid the finance company. That's the meaning of floorplanning. It has nothing to do with how the cars are displayed on the selling floor.

later had my bypass operation in 1988, she really worked behind-the-scenes and in a very low-key way to make sure that the company didn't miss a beat.

> *"When a boss becomes seriously ill, it's up to his or her assistant to anticipate what needs to be done, such as rerouting mail, spotting the issues the assistant or others are capable of handling, and following through. To do this well, you need to have a trusting boss who gives you confidence and shares information in the first place. Jim Moran is trust personified."*
>
> — *Marilyn Boesken*
> *Retired Assistant to the*
> *Chairman of the Board,*
> *JM Family*

This was the first time that I truly had a chance to build a dealership from the ground up, and I spared no pains to build it right. We conducted exhaustive soil tests, and the land was literally cleared tree stump by tree stump. Just on instinct, we made 119 design changes during the construction of the Pontiac dealership. It opened its doors on February 23, 1970, before the facility was fully finished. Both Herb Tousley and Marilyn spent many months walking around in hardhats during those days. Over its history, this store was the largest Pontiac dealership in the world. But a series of coincidences beginning the latter half of 1968 had started shifting my attention. A snowballing distraction was turning my head. For the first time in nearly 25 years, my foremost role in life was *not* going to be that of a car dealer...and the primary brand that I would be representing would *not* be a creation of Detroit's Big Three.

6

10,000 Toyotas

1968–1980

In 1968, while the first Pontiac dealership was being built in Homestead,[17] a friend in Chicago called and told me that Toyota was looking for a distributor in the Southeast United States and that Toyota was interested in talking to me. My response was, "What is a Toyota?"

If you had asked that very same question back in Japan in the 1920s, people would likely have said: "Well, a Toyota is an automatic loom." Sakichi Toyoda was a remarkable inventor of 84 devices, but his great claim to fame was an automatic loom. Kiichiro, Sakichi's son, really put the family into the motorcar business, and in 1937 he constructed the first plant in what is today called Toyota City in Nagoya. (Toyoda has 10 strokes in Japanese calligraphy, but the name was changed to Toyota for the car company because Toyota has eight strokes and eight is a lucky number in Japan, signifying prosperity. It was a better name for a consumer product.) Back before World War II, General Motors and Ford—believe it or not—

---

[17]Eventually the Pontiac dealership was sold as we focused our energies on our core businesses.

were a major factor in automobile manufacturing in Japan having 90% of the car business!

During the War, Toyota built trucks. Toward War's end, the firm even made a truck with one headlight in the very center of the hood, to conserve scarce parts. When peace arrived, the company was initially barred from producing cars or trucks because it had manufactured military vehicles. For a time, company divisions were even making chinaware and fish paste. But, Toyota was back making vehicles by the early fifties. After an unsuccessful attempt to enter the U.S. market in the late fifties, Toyota came back to the U.S. in the early sixties and was establishing a very small foothold.

In my immediate area, there was only one Toyota dealership and that was in Miami Beach, selling five to six cars a month. My initial conversations concerned a distributorship covering a 10-state territory. I told the liaisons with Toyota that GM was very good to me and no thank you. The friend in Chicago persisted, trying to find the right way to whet my appetite. Finally, he suggested that I drive a Toyota. About a week later, I did.

The first Toyota I drove was a red, stick-shift Corona[18] RT-52 Coupé. The styling was boxy and the car had neither power steering, radio, nor air conditioning. I took it out on I-95 and did everything to that car that I could, including throwing it into reverse at 55 MPH. The transmission didn't burn up. That the driveshaft stayed in place was nothing short of amazing. I never drove a car that was a better balanced vehicle. If quality problems were the bane of the U.S. automotive industry and pricey European imports were out of reach for the average consumer, here was a rugged, attractively priced car destined to revolutionize auto retailing in America. One drive and I was a believer.

---

[18] Corona, Corolla, Crown, Camry... It doesn't take a genius to figure out that there's a certain pattern to the beginning of many of Toyota's model names. For an interesting discussion of the reason why, see Eiji Toyoda's book: *Toyota: Fifty Years in Motion.*[1]

Conversations continued, and I then learned that Toyota had identified two other viable and interested candidates. The matter would now have to be decided in Japan. Toyota asked for a financial forecast. A member of my staff thought that I might win out if I made a strong pitch to Japan. Hal Barkun spent weeks readying the presentation. First, he approached outside help to do it. These consultants wanted an even longer time frame and demanded a hefty price tag: Eight weeks and $20,000! I said no to that. In the end, we did it ourselves and for less than $1,500. Toyota wanted to know everything, and Hal personally pounded out sheet after sheet of details at the typewriter. Every little nit on income and investment imaginable. We ended up with a book as thick as my wrist and put it into a handcrafted leather binding with the name of each member of Toyota's evaluation committee engraved on the cover. The shipping postage alone to get it to Japan as fast as we could was a huge $84, which was not a bad weekly salary for an administrator in Florida back then.

Two weeks later I got a call from Mr. Seisi Kato, who was then 59 and Executive Vice President of Toyota Motor Sales (TMS). He said that he would meet me at the Dupont Plaza Hotel in Miami Beach. I liked Kato immediately. After we spent an hour together, he asked me to take him out to the dealership in Homestead and then to show him the one I was building in Hollywood. Homestead befuddled him. "Why would you sell cars here?" he asked. I said to him that there were people all over, 15 miles this way and 20 miles that way. He was astonished.[19] He was more impressed with the site under construction in Hollywood.

---

[19] Large trading areas for dealerships were like life on another planet for the Japanese. Japan's habitable land is so densely populated—everything is concentrated. And retail distribution is totally different. Japan has large area dealers with small satellite offices in their territories. Although auto marketing in Japan is becoming more like that in the U.S., some cars in Japan are still sold by salespeople—armed with pictures of the various models available—making house calls.

Coming back on the return trip in my Pontiac, Mr. Kato sat in the front seat and looked straight ahead. Then, he asked me what turned out to be the critical question: "What would you do, Moran-san, if I shipped you ten thousand cars?" I gave him the only answer that I could think of: "I'd sell them." In disbelief, he turned to me asking, "What did you say?" Again, I told him that I would sell them, and you could see a smile break through on his face. It was to prove to be another risk-taking milestone for me. When you have conviction and confidence that you can do the deal, put yourself on the line first before somebody else does. As the great Chicago Cubs manager Leo Durocher used to put it: "You don't save a pitcher for tomorrow. Tomorrow it may rain."[m]

After my "ten-thousand-car" answer, I talked with Mr. Ohno—a Toyota Senior Managing Director who had accompanied Mr. Kato on the trip—and asked about the 10 states. Ohno said it would probably be five states with 40 dealers, selling a total of 300 to 400 cars per month. As we went on talking, Mr. Ohno was very cautious. Quietly I pressed him, but I could only get him to nod answers to three questions. Yes, Mr. Kato was impressed with what he saw …yes, he thought I would make a good distributor …no, Mr Kato didn't like the other two distributor candidates as much as he did me. Later on, Seisi Kato became one of my best friends, and he told me that the day on the freeway did it.

I said to Ohno that I was at a crucial point with the Pontiac dealership. He said that I really didn't need to invest so much with Toyota: He saw that investment as being in three parts: office space, some working capital, and a "floor plan" (as I've mentioned earlier, this is the auto retailing term describing the investment a distributor or dealer must make in its inventory of cars) of three million dollars, which included a liberal cushion above a minimum of $500,000.

About a week later, I got a telegram from Shotaro Kamiya, President of Toyota Motor Sales (TMS) saying that I had been selected as the distributor for five states—Florida,

North Carolina, South Carolina, Alabama, and Georgia. He asked if I could meet him in Tokyo at the Bank of Tokyo to sign the franchise. My franchise agreement with Toyota was signed in Japan on October 26, 1968. I was really taken with Shotaro Kamiya. He was four feet ten inches tall and weighed perhaps 90 pounds. When he met me, some kind of father-son relationship took hold. He had sons, but for all the years that he was alive, he called me his son. We had such similar thoughts about marketing, and I learned much from him about Japanese factories and customs. He was literally revered in Japan, where they called him the "God of Sales."

> *"What the Japanese have taught us has certainly benefitted the American car industry long-term, and my old friends back in Pontiac have told me just that."*
>
> *—Ed Dalton*
> *Retired Senior Vice President*
> *and General Manager,*
> *Southeast Toyota Part Processing*

Southeast Toyota is a distributorship for the third largest auto manufacturer in the world. Southeast Toyota does not own a Toyota dealership, but it supplies dealerships. I had no experience as a distributor. I understood and still understand the business from the customer's and the dealer's standpoint. I respected dealers and wanted to treat them as I had wanted to be treated as a dealer myself but never was. My goals were to take care of their needs and most of all to make them profitable.

TELL IT LIKE IT IS

"The Trick to Global Business is No Trick"

We have a good rapport with our Japanese friends at Toyota Headquarters in Nagoya. With all the hostility and distrust that seems to exist between Japanese and Americans on business issues, people ask me, "How do you *do* it?" Down deep, I guess I *do* know, and it's pretty simple: We share the same values, and the foremost values are honesty and loyalty.

It all begins with honesty about doing your job. Fifteen minutes after I signed our Toyota distributorship contract with Mr. Seisi Kato, then Executive Vice President of Toyota Motor Sales, he shook my hand and said: "Now, Moran-san... let's see some results."

We've always been honest about the results, whether they were good or bad. And we've tried very hard to show Toyota great results. If you're working with an overseas partner, you have to realize that basic performance measures carry far *more* weight than they do when your business partner is in the same country. If things are going right, there's not much to explain.

You have to produce the sales and profits that you say you will. Yes, floods, hurricanes, management turnover, a competitor's jillion-dollar sales event, or newspaper strikes can disrupt your business—but you have to do your best to anticipate problems and work around them. Otherwise, you spend plenty of time explaining "extenuating circumstances" long distance to people who try to understand what it all means, but may not really be able to do so.

Early in our relationship, the Japanese respected me when I pointed out that we would benefit from making headway in parts supply and distribution in the United States. That was over two decades ago, and now Toyota has the best parts-distribution system in the world—no one even comes close. Even back then, I followed some very good advice. At a meeting in which I gave Toyota management some bad news, I started out by praising all the many things that were *right* about Toyota. Then I got into the issues. The lesson: NEVER BEGIN A CONVERSATION WITH JAPANESE EXECUTIVES BY COMPLAINING. In the Japanese culture, leading off with negatives is considered arrogant, rude, and not constructive. So it's honesty…in a positive framework.

Two other values that we and the Japanese share are a commitment to excellence and a belief in equality. It may sound strange to link those two ideas, but I believe that they *are* linked. We have a saying in our companies: Nobody remembers number two. It means this: We're determined to be the best in every business in which we compete. That's how we describe excellence. However, inside of our businesses, we try very hard to steer away from "number ones". You're as likely to see a maintenance person flying on one of our corporate jets as you are an executive vice president. Just as in Japan, the plant manager and the assembly-line Associates wear the same white coveralls.

Our work ethics and views of loyalty are also a great match. Our people do what's needed to get the job done. Associates at our computer subsidiary often install data-processing systems for our dealers on weekends to disrupt the back-office operations in our dealerships the least. Not what's easiest for the Associate, but what's best for the business. We now even have a *Kaizen* (or, "continuous improvement") engineer in our Port Processing Center to help us design the best possible work flow.

Another point that may sound petty but really isn't: Japanese business hospitality is world famous, but I'm surprised at how few American firms doing regular business with the Japanese truly try to make Japanese executives feel at home when they come to the United States. At our Florida jet hangar, the first thing that a landing visitor sees are Japanese style gardens bordering the tarmac with a Japanese stone lantern. Often our people will assemble out front to applaud and greet guests as they arrive, just as our Japanese hosts applaud us when we go to Japan. The award-winning architecture of our buildings was designed to make guests from the East feel at home, and a Japanese architect came over to landscape the interior courtyard—a beautifully manicured rock garden, flanked by a display with an 800-year-old stone lantern. Best of all, our corporate chef, Richard Dezaki, can whip up some pretty good sashimi.

We share values and basic honesty; we believe in people first and loyalty.

We do not behave wholesale. We behave and believe retail. I wanted top quality training and marketing to sell new and used cars. I wanted the wherewithal to support dealers in the finance and insurance businesses and in parts and accessories, but only as a partner, giving them bigger percentages than they would have gotten from the domestics. I especially wanted to create a television marketing program—co-funded by the distributor and the dealerships—that would really register. Today, we also have a professionally staffed training program that outdistances what most distributorships offer.

With the Japanese, I felt that I had met brothers on issues like training and quality. When I was a kid, Japanese products were notorious for their cheapness and poor durability. Japanese was synonymous with disposable back then, but is that verdict ever wrong now! When I visited Toyota City in Nagoya, I was overwhelmed by the orderliness of the factory and the diligence of the Associates. The workers on the assembly line wore white gloves and no belt buckles while building the cars. Also, compared with my visits to Detroit, I had never seen such a level of worker/management communication as I did in Japan.

My first visit to Toyota City occurred not long after a very moving episode in that plant's history. To understand how deeply it hit home for me, a little background comparing the U.S. and Japanese auto industries may help. In an American plant producing 500 cars a day, you might see three people installing windshields. A Japanese plant with similar output would have one. At a Toyota plant in Nagoya, the windshield installer had been plying his craft for 15 years. One day, he cracked a windshield—his first. He was devastated and literally fled to his home out of shame.

The plant's managing director was concerned that the windshield installer might perform the *seppuku* ritual and do away with himself. The manager visited the Associate's home. He pleaded with the craftsman to come back and did everything possible to enable the person to save face. Fortunately he was able to bring the installer back and shifted the burden to the company from the humiliated Associate. In an American plant of the time, the worker would likely have filed a grievance with his shop steward and tried to pin the blame on the company...while management would be pointing its finger at the worker. Those fundamental differences in attitude between Japan and America underpinned the vast gap in quality between the cars of the two countries.

At the very beginning, Toyota and I were of a single mind on quality and work standards...and light years apart on styling. "What is all this that Jim Moran keeps preaching about styling?" I'm sure that's what the Japanese in Nagoya kept thinking. Even today, a car in Japan is a *personal utility*. Overall, domestic cars in Japan have been narrower, slower, simpler, and equipped with only the most basic options. The differences in car preferences between the two countries are declining; but, in the United States, people still want cars to make a stronger personal statement about themselves. The cars we buy are generally more powerful and have a host of visual features and comfortable conveniences.

Beginning in the late sixties, we strongly suggested that the Japanese put in something other than a black interior. They came out with a brown-beige interior with five different shades of brown. They couldn't understand why this was not acceptable to women car buyers. And, they offered these colors while still coupling the choices with a black dashboard and steering wheel!

While styling was initially a struggle—and a topic I'll come back to a little later—my first priority was not the cars but the service and the parts availability that make prompt service possible. That system had to be in place before we ever really merchandised the cars aggressively. After I was a distributor for two months, I was startled to learn that there were few parts available in the United States. As I said earlier, *for a dealer, there is one thing worse than not putting cars on the road, and that is putting cars on the road that you can't service*. I did not want to see the Renault catastrophe of the Courtesy Ford era repeated. In the auto business, you can sell a customer once, but if that customer has problems getting a replacement part for their car, odds are high that they won't be back again. The part may be something as simple as a water pump or even a certain kind of cotter key, but the car could become unusable.

Through opinion samplings taken around this time, the American public was saying that they would like to buy an import car, but it was a problem to get it fixed. VW mastered this problem first. If we wanted to surpass brands like VW, we had to do a great job on parts.

Toyota was then trying to supply parts for the entire East Coast of the United States out of a parts depot in Engleside Cliffs, New Jersey. When we signed a dealer, they could get $1,500 worth of Toyota Land Cruiser parts and we weren't selling many Land Cruisers. The person whom I turned to in solving this complex challenge was Bob France. Bob was actually the first Associate hired. He joined us from Jeep where he managed several small, but very efficient parts depots. Bob really had a "can-do" attitude! "We don't go home until the parts are sent to the customer" was his outlook every day. Bob made a real difference.[20]

Today you couldn't dream of a more ideal relationship between manufacturer and distributor than the one that exists between Southeast Toyota and TMS in Torrance, California. It's been like that for decades. Back then, however, the first years were rocky; and the parts system was so important. Our joint success in perfecting a parts system was a major step in drawing us together. Volkswagen, as was pointed out, was able to achieve what it did as an import because it had one of the best parts systems in the country. To beat VW, a breakthrough on Toyota parts distribution was crucial. We recommended a professional parts inventory control system, the establishment of parts depots around the country,

---

[20] Back at that time, we were selling thirty to forty thousand dollars worth of parts a month. Today we sell as much as twenty-one *million* dollars worth of parts a month!

and on-line computer support for dealer parts ordering. Toyota approved the warehouses and an ordering system, but not the inventory control system.

We went ahead and computerized dealer parts inventory control on our own and were the only factory or distributor to do so. This was in 1969 on a base of 42 dealers. We set up a data line that allowed dealerships to report regularly what parts and accessories they needed. We computerized parts inventory control before Ford and GM did. The computer analyzed each parts transaction and set up replenishment levels daily.

TMS applied our parts system principles throughout the United States. Toyota's parts performance is now one of the most efficient in the world. After three or four years we were able to fill an order on first pass over 95 percent of the time as both our sales volume and as the actual number of parts (presently it's about 50,000) grew sharply.

The parts breakthrough had an even deeper impact on me. Southeast Toyota—we concluded—had to become the standard setter in every other area that could be systematized: *That included port processing of vehicles, computerization, accessorizing the cars, financing and after-market sales, and training.* This attitude caused us to take a far more sophisticated and professional approach to managing the distributorship at a very early time. As a result, we and our dealers have reaped enormous rewards for more than two decades.

To serve the dealerships in Mobile, Tampa, Charlotte and all the other locations effectively, our first priority became making our facilities in Jacksonville the best and the most reliable that they could be. In this chapter, I'll talk about our early efforts in perfecting those facilities, but I'll come back to their current operation in chapter 7 because they really are the heartbeat of our integrated marketing approach today.

For an import distributor, everything starts at the port. Toyota had already established Jacksonville as the entry port. We were anxious to create a port operation of our own, as other distributors had done, and Toyota supported us in this. Later, Toyota itself adopted many of the practices pioneered in port management and processing at Jacksonville.

The original Jacksonville port we took over was impossible. It consisted of some leased property under the spans of the Matthews Bridge. Stevedores were hired to unload the boats. The parking places were up to the cars' hubs in mud and debris. At night, bums would break open car doors and sleep in the vehicles. The cars were littered with pop bottles and half-eaten hot-dog buns. Today—and for years—experts tell us that we have had the best managed port facility for any auto company (bar none) in efficiency, quality, and timeliness.

"Jim Moran is a humble man and caring man, who knows how to put his wherewithal to good use, and I can think of two demonstrations of this. JM Family has had a pivotal impact on employment opportunities for African-American and other disenfranchised individuals, particularly in the Jacksonville Port district. And, its African-American Achiever Awards are a pioneering model that the business community could emulate. I don't know of a businessman anywhere who shares his success more readily and graciously than Jim Moran!"

—Dr. Richard Danford
President,
Jacksonville, Urban League

In Jacksonville, we found an old abandoned Ford Model-T assembly plant. (There was to be no getting away from Ford, was there?) When we started, an outside company processed the cars and they would unload cars that stayed on the dock for seven days. The longshoremen were not trained to move the cars properly. The owner of the plant, who used to process the cars too, tried to double our rent shortly after we signed on with Toyota. So we negotiated for a new site with the Jacksonville Port Authority.

Southeast Toyota Port Processing is 15 miles inland on the St. John's River, a waterway which is linked directly with the Atlantic Ocean. Our dock is 720 feet long. The first headquarters there opened in 1972 and today the complex occupies 270,000 square feet of buildings over 70 acres. On an average day, the team there can completely process, accessorize, and equip 630 vehicles.

Constructing the Port Processing Center and the parts depot required an enormous investment from us at the time—the biggest investment that I had ever made in my life. The first parts building cost over two and a half million dollars. Its later replacement was far more expensive, but some good financing enabled us to build the bigger and more automated facility later in Deerwood Center. This investment came long before we left our tiny South Florida offices on McNab road in Pompano Beach to move to the much bigger offices in Deerfield Beach, because I wanted the investment in port facilities, parts, systems, training, and vehicle processing to be made first and to be the best possible.

The Jacksonville facilities are the core of our business as a distributor, and that's why I traveled constantly to Jacksonville when those facilities were first being constructed. But we had to move a mountain to do it right. You think I'm joking, but we literally had to move ONE WHOLE MOUNTAIN—Mt. Kennelly—to build our facilities. At first, the Port Authority said forget it...this was out of the question. In truth, Mt. Kennelly was really a big hill—two and a half million cubic yards of dirt. When we bought property across the street and suggested that we might opt for this as yet another site, we let the Authority know that we were serious. They finally conceded, when we showed them that our correctly developed property would be worth millions in jobs and value in a few years.

Just where do you put a mountain when you want to move it? George Herbert—who had worked with me at Courtesy Motors in Chicago—suggested that we haul the mountain into areas where dirt was needed. In 18 months, it was done. Then we built our facility piece by piece.

"Some companies are profit-driven. Others are market-ing-driven. We like to think that ours is improvement-driven."

— L. Wayne McClain
Executive Vice President
Administration,
JM Family

In the early seventies, George Herbert engineered and constructed the first environmentally-sound wash rack in the U.S., and it could remove the shipping coating from 200 to 300 cars a day. We no longer had people hand-cleaning cars with kerosene.

Ed Dalton, who had spent 29 years with Pontiac and retired as that company's Assistant Production Manager, first studied our processing facilities as a consultant. Southeast Toyota Port Processing became a genuine plant—just like our Courtesy Conditioning operation in Chicago. Ed established a quality-control system for processing that became a standard for the industry.

Steadily, we made progress. In 1973 Southeast Toyota outregistered Volkswagen—which was then both the dominant small car force and the leading import—in the Southeast for the first time. This breakthrough would not occur in the rest of the United States until some years later.

Toyota was still criticized for its styling, but the car was very well built. And it offered economy *and* price at about $1,500. We were making breakthroughs in the processing, but a lot of work still needed to be done on the *styling* if Toyota was to really make it in the American market. We tried very hard to think of ways to get around the styling challenge. Customization seemed the only short-term solution, and Dick Knox helped me tackle the styling. My instinct for customizing cars goes all the way back to the Baby Hornet; except today, we have come so far that the computer helps us plan it and we implement it through actual production lines. The first Toyota cars in the United States were color-blind, not color-coordinated. When we started importing, we got cars in blue, white, and red...and none of them metallic paints. If you have six red, six blue and six white, and they're all equipped the same way, you are offering the customer only three choices. But, with creative accessorization, you can present customers a multitude of choices that could help make up for the dull styling and color options. Why not do it?

Our first steps were modest. We developed vinyl tops and luggage racks. Later we created an accessory assembly line. We wanted these wonderful boxy cars to be sexier, so we brought in a styling engineer during the late seventies to create a line of modified Toyotas with a futuristic look. We came up with a model called the "Sun Chaser" and one called the "Tiger". We called this line of cars "Future Cars", and it included a Woodie-style wagon called the "Honcho". We even registered the trademark and when American Motors later came out with a "Honcho" of their own, they paid us $250,000 to use the name.

These cars set an image of what we thought a Toyota could look like in the future. We redid the paint, the color coordination, the air dams, and the front end. Even though we had our own car shows as a distributorship, we could never produce our "limited editions" in any volume. When we put them on display for the dealers, they went wild; the cars we customized sold like hot cakes. It was all cosmetic customization. We never touched the mechanical parts of the car.

"When the Previa was designed, we took a Toyota engineering team to an elementary school and talked to the principal on Jim Moran's suggestion. 'Make those doors lighter,' she declared! 'A kid who weighs forty pounds can't shove a door that weighs sixty.' We're trained to always have our heads up looking for insights like that."

—Darryl Head
Director, Enterprise Architecture Planning
JM Family

We also improved car styling and profitability by putting trim rings and covers on the wheels. We innovated by manufacturing our own steel alloy wheels. In accessories, we went out and asked people like Carol Shelby of Ford-Shelby GT fame to design the wheels and other elements. Roger Chastain worked with us for years. Sometimes all that was needed was a minor touch like rounding the finish on a square corner or coloring the inside of the wheel. A tiny nuance could make all the difference in the world. Today, with computer-aided design you can do so much. So much better than the wood, putty, and clay we had to play with back then.

Toyota's styling is outstanding now, but we still do some adaptations to match what we feel are the tastes of the American consumer. When I saw the first mock-up of the 1990 Celica, we knew immediately that the car needed a spoiler. The bulbous rear-end with its large spacing above the rear wheel and the small spacing above the front just wouldn't hit the eye of the American customer in the right way, we thought. When that Celica model came out in the fall of 1989, its sales didn't take off as fast as hoped. However once we spruced it up with a little flair, we went right through our inventory in days. We came up with a package called the *STX* that included a rear spoiler, special wheels, upgraded tires, emblems, and painted mirrors. It made such a dramatic change in the car that it gave us 20 percent of the national Celica market. In 1991, when we previewed the new Camry in Japan, we decided it needed gold trim. We sold 12,000 gold packages in 1993—replacing the badging. The gold emblems—paired with European-styled wheels—sold more strongly than we expected.[21] The Camry moved up into the Lexus line. Customers love the class it adds.

---

[21] Japanese manufactured Toyotas have a tire size of 13-14 inches, much smaller than Americans like. We change some of the wheels that come in from Japan and sell the take-off wheels in Sweden because Sweden has a mandatory snowtire law during the winter, and Swedes like to keep the tires mounted on a spare set of wheels.

"Southeast Toyota recently launched a leather interior option on the Camry. The leather option had been such a popular success for Courtesy in Chicago. It's amazing how quality customization options endure."

—Gary Hall
Former Group Vice President
Southeast Toyota Port Processing

On my early trips to Japan, I tried to persuade Toyota to build an upscale car. They had one for the domestic market called the "Crown", and it was the first Toyota model of any sort that they attempted to test-market as an export to the United States. The first Crowns arrived in 1957, but they proved to be a failure in our market. For one thing, the car was too narrow and under-powered for a luxury-class auto on freeways. Toyota ended up bringing the cars back to Japan.

Twelve years ago, Dr. Toyoda came to visit us in Deerfield Beach. After touring our new headquarters facility, he said that he wanted to talk about car design. I was happy he opened up the topic. We sat down in our boardroom, and I told him, "Why don't we offer a luxury car, a car with luxury, quality, and a prestige image? We've mastered everything else in the automotive business. We have the best quality. We have the best engines. We have great styling. Something like the Crown, which is the most successful luxury car in Japan, but a car truly designed for the American market. A Crown-*like* car for the United States. We can make the finest luxury car in the world at Toyota."

He asked me how many we could sell. I said 30,000 in the first year and 60,000 in the second. He wanted to know more about the specs. I said it would have to be a full-size car, able to seat five passengers comfortably with plenty of head and seat room, with a V-8 engine, superior styling, better quality than anybody else, and the backup of exceptional service. We at Southeast Toyota also felt that Japan's image was *quality* cars but not yet *luxury* cars. Dr. Toyoda, who is an engineer, kept on digging for what else such a car would need. I said, "It has to have rear-wheel drive." Dr. Toyoda paused for a moment. "I think like Moran-san does," was all he said. That discussion was one of the seeds that launched the Lexus. When Dr. Toyoda returned to Japan, Toyota made a commitment and gave its Chief of Product Development Mr. Sasaki and Lexus Chief Engineer Mr. Suzuki a billion dollars to work with and told them to build the best luxury car in the world.

Success has many fathers and many birthplaces, but I think I'm fair in saying that this discussion in a Deerfield Beach conference room contributed to the creation of one of the great success stories in automotive history—the Lexus. Five years later, the first one rolled onto the shores of America. It would have been unimaginable in my Hudson or Ford days for a dealer or distributor to have exerted as much influence on the design of a car. *The Japanese know that an experienced and successful marketer never speaks with his own voice but with the voice of the customer.*

> "Jim Moran was Toyota's great teacher of auto marketing in the United States. He has both product and marketing knowledge to a remarkable degree. Frankly, Jim is the best retail guy I've ever met in over forty years in the business."
>
> — Bob McCurry
> Retired Vice Chairman,
> Toyota Motor Sales, USA

There is no luxury car in the world like a Lexus. No European nameplate is its equal; and, since its inception, it has outsold the Nissan Infiniti two-to-one. Toyota took painstaking care to define the Lexus as a totally separate brand right down to the selling floor where it's sold. Even though Toyota showrooms are some of the finest around, the Lexus showroom is a study in elegance with its regal floors and tinted glass. The private sales areas have video monitors and VCRs for prospects to view tapes on the various models, colors, and performance and feature highlights. On the rare occasion that a Lexus is brought in for service, the owner drives out with an immediate loaner. JM Family Enterprises owns the largest and most successful Lexus dealership in the United States. Lexus also continues to be the wellspring for many innovations—like the laminated metal firewall under the dashboard—which are now standard for mainline Toyotas. The bottom line may tell the story best. Lexus accounts for two percent of Toyota's unit sales and a third of its profits.[n]

As I've said in chapter 4, advertising cannot be a gimmick. It must be believable. That's the first and foremost criterion. Second, marketers have to ask themselves: Does the ad give the viewer or reader *positive* information? Facts on which to act. *An ad must resolve more questions for the customer than are raised.* You build customer confidence in small deliberate steps—not with showy pledges. Tell it like it is on: price, features, accessories...and the deal.

Toyota ranks high on the list of the top 100 national advertisers in the U.S. with a major presence on TV each year. SET annually spends thirty million dollars for its five-state region's own advertising. Dealerships themselves may also spend from $20,000 to $150,000 a month depending on size. In a few cases, a dealer may even spend $200,000 in some months. The ad budget is in synch with the timing of how vehicles are distributed, and distribution follows the seasonal buying peaks of customers. Basically, you let history tell you when you're going to sell many cars and when you won't. More money is spent from March into the summer than in January or February. There's also generally a large promotion at year-end in December.

Folks tend to think that all the Toyota advertising comes from a single source—one great big national or perhaps even international campaign. In practice, things work differently. TMS, USA (Toyota Motor Sales, USA) focuses on *product* advertising that explains the features of cars and introduces new models. It's aimed at positioning Toyota as a brand and as an image for the consumer.

The national advertising also sends home a slogan or theme that consumers will instantly associate with Toyota. The great Toyota campaigns probably began with: "Get your hands on a Toyota. You'll never let go." That one really helped Toyota make its mark in the United States in the early seventies. Then: "You asked for it. You got it," which launched the '76 car.

That campaign lasted for a long time. The theme now is "I love what you do for me." Three times a year, TMS has "thrust months" when they know that their inventory will be at a peak. March, July, and December are typical thrust months. TMS moves away from the product angle during these times and dealers across the country participate in nationwide sales events.

In the car business, there's no substitute for a trustworthy endorsement of quality. I mentioned that point in my recollections of Hudson advertising back in chapter 3 and how I may have been seen as a "quality spokesperson" for used cars. That's why Toyota often references the results of the eminent J.D. Power studies.

The results of these studies confer the leading seal of approval in the auto industry. Scan these excerpts from national advertising for Toyota trucks in 1995, based on J.D. Power findings:

- Toyota—#1 Truckline in Initial Quality
- Toyota Compact Truck—Best Compact Pickup in Initial Quality
- 4Runner—Best Compact Sport Utility in Initial Quality
- Previa—Best Compact Van in Initial Quality
- T100—Best Full-Size Pickup in Initial Quality

HOW CAN YOU SAY MORE OR BETTER?

In comparison to brand-building ads like that one nationally, local sales events and specials are the constant and almost sole purpose of distributor and dealer advertising. Said straight and simple: It's the job of TMS to invite people to consider the brand and the job of SET and its dealers to give them good reasons to come in and buy now.

Although I'm not an on-camera spokesperson doing TV ads any more, I'm still very much in the thick of designing ad campaigns for the distributorship. (Toyota, by the way, wouldn't have an objection if I were on television, but it wouldn't make sense since I'm a distributor and not a dealer.)

> *"When our team turned World Cars into a profit maker, we did it by performing up to a single standard: Quality is the only thing we have for sale. Jim Moran believed in the principle and so did we."*
>
> *—Vic McNair*
> *Retired Executive Vice President*
> *and General Manager, World Cars*

At SET, we used to be small enough so that three or four of us could get together and toss around a marketing idea. But size has caused us to organize and schedule our meetings more now, and that's too bad. Thank God that we do not have the stuffy cycle of "marketing planning meetings" that strangle typical corporations. If and when we ever do, I'll know that it's time to hang up my spurs. Jim Moran, Jr., played an important role in the evolution of our marketing program. Jim is really attuned to the media end of the business. He bought exposure efficiently and got us an excellent return for our media investment. Additionally, he has a knack for sparking a creative concept. Jim also has a personal flair that came across especially well when he emceed large-scale incentive events, doing so with great humor.

After Hal Barkun retired, Dick Kelly became an excellent source of advertising advice for me. I first met Dick when he was with the Clinton E. Frank Agency in Chicago in the early seventies. He then worked with Dancer Fitzgerald and Sample—which has since become a part of Southeast Toyota's current agency Saatchi & Saatchi. Dick has always been a creative guy and a good organizer.

If SET has been an innovator in advertising, it's been with two concepts: Toyotathons and tent sales.

We did our first Toyotathon in 1976. It added some important twists to the "sellathon" concept. Marketing experts define "sellathon" as a non-stop 24-hour sale. No one had tried such a big-scale selling event that tied in independent dealers hundreds and hundreds of miles away.

In the first Toyotathon, every dealer in the five-state distributorship was open for 72 hours straight! When I started the logistics plan, I thought we were mobilizing for D-Day II. Searchlights scanning the skies, cots on the showroom floors, sleep-shifts and "watches" for customers, catered food for the sales Associates, morale-building phone calls, and performance contests. We consciously used all the extra TV time that was being bought to attract customers, to also boost inside awareness of the Toyotathon's importance among our dealers and their salespeople.

"The energy and excitement of our first Toyotathon was incredible. One gigantic sales event...and it worked! Dealers had wall-to-wall traffic and record sales for the weekend."

> *—Dick Kelly*
> *Retired Advertising Manager,*
> *SET*

We still run two Toyotathons a year at SET, but the concept has changed. As with any concept, customers become accustomed to it; and there's no burning reason any more to be open for 72 hours straight. Today, we keep the Toyotathon name—and all the positive triggers that go with it—but we spread the timespan over two to three weeks. Not long after our first successes, TMS picked up the Toyotathon idea, using their own names like "Clock-stopping, super-shopping time." Were we miffed that TMS adopted the program? Of course not! If we weren't creative and willing to experiment, why would they need us as a distributor?

Too many non-factory distributorships in industries of all kinds feel just the opposite. They think that *factory-owned distributors* should set the innovation standard. That's a key reason why so few creative things get done in business.

Tent sales were another of our innovations in the vehicle market place. When we did *our* first tent sale, our cars were in especially short supply. An off-site sale doesn't make sense if you don't have the inventory. But, at that point we had trucks! We had more trucks than we knew what to do with.

If you're going to sell trucks, think country-and-western, because that's what many truck customers like. We rolled out the "Truck Rodeo" sale. Salespeople wore cowboy hats. The music and the style of the ads couldn't have been more down-home country-and-western. We used Tampa Stadium as our staging area. It was the first time anyone had put 800 trucks in a stadium. Ten dealers took part in this three-day offsite sale. We blitzed television. We did 15 more similar rodeos in different markets over the next 12 months.

In a tent sale, the tent itself is where the business is done. What makes a tent sale special is the huge assortment available—the bigness and the selection. It was a new way of buying cars and trucks, and—even though the vehicle was sold in the middle of a stadium—you could still drive off with what you bought that same day.

My friend Dr. David Fry is the distinguished President of Northwood University (an educational mecca for the entire automobile industry) and an educated observer of the automotive scene. David describes tent sales as "massing product, supermarket style." Dealers jointly participated in running the event and kept their dealerships open too. When the concept was fresh, the success was colossal; but a tent sale is grueling work. Motivation can easily wane. It's not like selling out of an air-conditioned showroom.

While the tent sale concept may have lost some of its gloss today, we staged the extravaganza of all tent sales with "The Monsoon Sale" in January 1988, when the concept was at its very peak. We called it "Operation Monsoon" because of the sheer volume of business we anticipated doing.

Mapping the battle plan for this event began an entire year before hand. This was the first time that we tried to orchestrate a massive off-site sale in *every* market in *all* five states all at once...and did so over a period of *10* days. We staged it at 21 different offsite locations—including Port Everglades, Joe Robbie Stadium, Tampa Stadium, the Jai Alai Fronton in Orlando, and Fulton County Stadium in Atlanta. It required eight million dollars in advertising and promotion costs. We sold over *12,000 vehicles* that month. It was a motivational marathon which had me helicoptering from point to point handing out cash bonuses to salespeople (all duly noted for the wage records by our accounting folks of course). There's no substitute for *visible management motivation* during a campaign like that.

The one great thing about promotions with fundamental value is that they never really die, even though they can fall out of fashion for a time. Wait about 10 or 20 years, and you can always revive a "golden oldie" with just a little updating and turn it into a hit. "Thanks a Million" was one such "re-tread". We did it to celebrate SET's millionth vehicle sale in 1985 as a joint effort with Sears. The idea was this: Buy a Toyota now, and you can have your choice of a series of big ticket items such as a washer, dryer, fishing boat, TV, or VCR. Readers may remember that the dealership used this very same attraction in the post-World War II Hudson days, during the era of appliance scarcities. Both times the results were stellar.

Toyota has used Squire Fridell as a spokesperson for various campaigns since 1979. He represents us three or four times a year. (Last year he was also a guest speaker at SET's 25th anniversary.) He's mature (but youngish looking), enthusiastic, energetic, genuine, believable. You may not know his name, but I'd be shocked if you wouldn't recognize him instantly if you saw him and just naturally like him. He's done a great deal of TV work, especially in comedies.

Marketing and advertising are the most important elements of auto retailing. *The leading competitor has to dominate the media that you are in and television is one of the best media.* The manufacturer has to deliver the product and public awareness of it. The dealer has to provide the price and the terms. For 27 years, Toyota Motor Sales and Southeast Toyota have probably had the best marketing marriage in the business to create exactly that.

> *"The Japanese have always thought of my Dad as the number-one American for retail input. They wanted to learn from successful, independent retailers, not factory people."*
>
> — *Jim Moran, Jr.*
> *Director,*
> *JM Family*

Fleet sales and the evolution of our own finance company were two other tools that helped us build sales volume. When Ted Pass joined us from GM/Pontiac, we were really able to develop our fleet sales. I guess the authorities define fleet sales as auto sales to any company in excess of any 10 vehicles for a given year. We knew—and I have to believe that Toyota knew, too—that if we were to get Toyotas into the hands of fleet-sales customers like rent-a-car companies, everyday people would soon come to appreciate the value of a Toyota. Southern Florida was and is one of the two biggest rental-car markets in the entire world. Because of the fleet-sales customers which Ted Pass and his team allowed us to develop, Toyota earned crucial national recognition and everyone was to benefit.

Hugh Woods was our choice to launch a finance company within JM Family Enterprises. He was a seasoned veteran of GMAC and understood auto finance. Hugh shared my confidence that we could successfully take the initial risk of more than thirty million dollars in retail customer debts, understanding that the repayments of those debts would dribble in monthly in installments. Hugh's sense for the right direction helped create the cornerstone of World Omni today—one of the greatest achievements in the JM Family group of companies.

It's been a wonderful marriage—Toyota and SET. The Japanese are always so conscious of doing the right thing. I'm sure we blundered a couple of times along the way. The fact that the Japanese don't have the word "no" in their language can make things difficult sometimes. You come away feeling that *you're* the super diplomat, when—in truth—*they* really are.[22]

Over the years, I've taken a number of international trips with John McNally. John was president during our early years of growth. His experience in international business made him well suited for starting up JM Family's General Motors distributorship in France called NAVI. Earlier, he was instrumental in forging a relationship with Toyota as our dealership body grew from 42 to approximately 160.

Not all my efforts at international diplomacy in Japan have worked equally well. One time John and I took a group of sales contest winners from the dealerships over to Japan. To show my appreciation for the wonderful hospitality we'd be receiving, I really wanted to make a speech in Japanese. One of the Japanese Toyota managers in California offered to translate my talk from English to Japanese and to record the speech in Japanese for me. For days, I rehearsed, studying the sounds on the tape.

I was going to surprise the audience, and boy did I! The speech started off with the Japanese version of: "Ladies and gentlemen, thank you for arranging this party." "Mensan koun-ban-woh potty woh arrangey" delivered with a Midwestern twang...and the translator turned ashen. He didn't know what I was saying, or maybe he hoped that I

---

[22] By the way, it is harder and harder to think of Toyota as really being a *Japanese* company. Toyota is doing an astonishing job in using domestic U.S. components. And, it is also such a substantial automobile manufacturer today in North America. Toyota is truly a multinational corporation.

didn't intend to say what he THOUGHT he was hearing.

The Japanese in the audience didn't understand what I was saying. The Americans didn't know what I was saying—but all of them were looking at the astonished faces of our Japanese hosts. My countrymen were pretty sure that whatever I was suggesting wasn't a very good idea. I spent all my time looking at the phonetic notes I had sketched, so I wasn't paying attention to the audience's reaction. My ordeal seemed to go on for an hour and a half, though it only lasted five minutes. At the end, the stunned translator looked over and asked: "*What* are you trying to say?"

I smiled apologetically and said, "Well, that's enough of that...please tell them how happy I am they are all here today."

7

Mega-Tech
Marketing

1980–Present

I'm sitting in a golf cart with Bob Moore. Bob was recently appointed Vice President of Vehicle Processing for our Port Processing Center. We're trying to use the visors of our Florida Seminole baseball caps to shield out the beating sun. Bob recently set up and ran our Inland Port Processing Facility in Commerce, Georgia. He came up through the management ranks and is following in the footsteps of his predecessor, Gary Hall, who did a fine job of building many of the systems that distinguish our port processing facility as a world-class operation. Dazzling is the only way to describe what technology allows us to accomplish in processing today. Bar-coding sensors can pinpoint the location of each vehicle as it moves through the Center. Sophisticated load processing systems decide the exact best order to prepare thousands of vehicles. And, space-age lasers etch security numbers into windshields.

We're parked on what's called *Moran's Landing*. I think it was so named because they figured that this is where I would end up, down-and-out, if this enormously expensive processing facility hadn't worked out. But, thanks to good luck and the hard work of the talented Associates in Jacksonville, it has proved to be a success.

The industry still can't believe that we can get cars from overseas to the dealers with less than two percent damage. In fact, the late W. Edwards Deming—the distinguished authority on Japanese management practices—suggested that Pontiac study what we were doing. They have and so have many others. But Southeast Toyota Port Processing and our parts operations just continue to get better all the time. You've heard something about this operation earlier. Some of the things we are doing there now are especially exciting.

Right now, we're watching the 11-story car carrier christened *Sunbelt Dixie* being unloaded at a rate of 500 cars per hour. They used to be lifted off in a car cradle ONE AT A TIME. The cars are driven off now after being fueled in Japan with just enough gas to get off the ship. It's a 24-day trip through the Panama Canal to Jacksonville. A car carrier docks in Jacksonville every Tuesday. The chairman of the company that owns and operates the *Sunbelt Dixie* credits me with the fact that several decks of the ship are used to carry fresh fruit from the United States back to Japan. Maybe this arrangement is a little help for our international balance of payments.

Ahead of the time the ship is unloaded, we tell the longshoremen where every single car is to go following a specific plan. A sticker that designates where it is to be parked is placed on the vehicle as it is being off-loaded in Jacksonville. After inspection, we fuel those cars that need to be prepared for delivery first. The parking area is a jumbo-sized grid. We use the computer to design how the grid itself is organized each day. One day a car-sized rectangle could be part of a drive path, the next day a holding area. We recently purchased an industrial engineering computer program that will help us process vehicles even better. It lets us visualize any changes that we want to make in how we move vehicles around Southeast Toyota Port Processing and to simulate those changes first.

Our first big improvement was to install a staging system that reduced the processing time (our experts say I should call it "velocity") from 10 days to six and a half days. Our newest system—Advance Load Processing—which we implemented in 1990 got us down to 2.8 days. It's the leading system in the country, and it has really enhanced our ability to make "truckable loads" or "shippable configurations"—a load full enough to be sent by truck. Why bother with all this planning? The cost of money was a major factor.

The scale of business on which we operate today has grown so much from our first years. When we started out, a shipload of cars was under a million dollars. In 1994 it ran as much as fifty to fifty-five million dollars, and the cars were paid for by wire transfer immediately upon passing customs.

Larry Rich is a very regular guy, but I still believe that he dozes off at night with a computer under his pillow. Larry figured out that every one-day reduction in processing time yielded an annual savings of $450,000 on inventory holding costs because of interest rates. Now we've shifted our attention to speeding up the processing of car and truck imports, and we're installing optical-scanning radio-frequency equipment that will tell us where each car is at a given moment and the ideal route it should take through the processing facility. Once a vehicle is on the road on an eighteen-wheeler, satellite beams will tell us its exact location until delivery. We have a 99.6 percent on-time delivery performance in getting cars to dealers today, but we hope to make that better.

Our golf cart is now parked in front of one of our two dynamometers. These simulate the car in motion and can tell in a flash if the cruise control works right and if the number on the speedometer matches the actual speed of the car up to 120 MPH. We now do a factory-authorized pre-delivery inspection centrally on 200 cars a day. The 46-point check includes seatbelts, leaks under the chassis, child-safety features, radio pre-settings, clock, spare tire, headlight aiming, and much more.

Our dealers are supplied from either Southeast Toyota Port Processing or the brand new 84,000-square-foot distribution center we built in Commerce, Georgia, erected on over 300 acres with its own railroad spurs and trucking center. John Hill manages the Commerce facility. Commerce basically supplies domestically produced cars for the northern zone of the distributorship. It's operated by only 71 Associates, but it processes between 55,000–60,000 cars a year. After you see the efficiency with which cars are prepped and accessorized at Commerce or Jacksonville, it's hard to imagine the primitive, old days when individual dealers tried to do this by themselves on a piecework basis. Our team at Commerce does a great job for all of us.

All the fancy technology at Southeast Toyota Port Processing still boggles my mind and maybe yours too, but I think we've achieved even more revolutionary results. We're really *doing* something with the Japanese management approaches that so many firms just talk about. We've put a number of *Kaizen*—continuous improvement—concepts to work for us. We hired a *Kaizen* engineer four years ago. He's important as a go-between, but the real breakthroughs are achieved by our Associates themselves.

Let me tell you about an important advance we made with a nasty beginning. Not long ago, one of our Associates fell off a welded rail-car ladder and broke his arm. All of us were sick about it. These ladders run 90 degrees straight up over a slick steel bar. Associates doing the unloading would have to climb to the top of a railcar on the third level and swing their body weight around to the open door, getting a foothold on the door to lower the bridge plate so the cars could be offloaded. If there's a little bit of sweat, rain, or grease, you can lose your footing.

The entire off-loading squad became a *Kaizen* team and met twice a week for about six weeks to figure out how we could solve the problem. This wasn't easy. For starters, all the "official" safety standards were already being met. But, that didn't stop our team. Through their work, we've designed a totally new method for unloading rail that includes a rolling staircase and a lock-on system with chains. It looks a little like an airline stepway. We owe a lot to *Kaizen*—especially when it keeps our team safe and healthy—but some of the other approaches have been a harder sell. We have tried organizing regular stretching calisthenics in the morning, but it's been a slow go.

Across town from our Port Processing Center in Jacksonville is our Parts Distribution Center. It sits behind a beautifully manicured lawn bordered by elegant shrubbery and plants. The setting looks more like that of an office park than a Parts Center. More than seven acres of parts (that's roughly the size of six football fields) with a value in excess of forty million dollars are kept in this center at any one time, but few stay there very long.

In 1994, the Parts operation shipped over $220 million worth of parts to dealers. The Associate team there just surpassed an all-time record in shipping a million dollars worth of parts to dealers in one day.

"When JM Family Enterprises was still pretty young, we knew that we had to attract some more top-notch people. Jim Moran asked me to propose some new programs to bolster our benefit package. I came back with seven or eight, figuring he might want to start with one or two. After I briefed him, he said 'Do it.' 'Which one?' I asked. 'Do 'em all. These are things that we should be doing.' I was floored. For an owner/entrepreneur that kind of investment in people was and is unheard of. We rolled out the entire package in just eighteen months. Today our profit-sharing and retirement accounts—which are completely company-funded by JM Family—have over $170 million in trust for our people at no cost to them."

— *Larry Rich*
Chief Operating Officer
and Director,
JM Family

There are only 47 Associates on the Parts floor and 26 of them in the office area (which is itself completely computerized), and that's a key point because it shows that modern distribution is as much a matter of moving information as it is moving product. Overtime is less than five percent a year, and almost all of the Associates work regular 40-hour weeks. Powerful equipment now handles all the back-breaking lifting that I remember from my days at the Graham Paper Company. The forklifts are all made by Toyota and are supplied through another of our companies— Southeast Industrial Equipment. They are equipped with two-way radio gear. Remembering the famous sleuth's two-way wristwatch radio, our Dick (or Debbie) Tracy will never have to leave his (or her) equipment to get a question answered. Orange floats roll by, hooked to a tugger like a miniature railroad. Moving as smoothly as giraffes, mechanical cherry pickers sweep up to nearly the top of the Center's 24-foot ceiling to snap hold of items. The sophisticated equipment gives you the impression the whole facility is driven by high-power machinery, but the single most powerful tool in the entire place is a simple adhesive label.

That label goes on every part shipment and truly drives everything. If you pick up a package in the outbound shipping section, you'll see a computerized label that contains— among other things—the parts description, its number, location, and a complete identification of the dealer who receives it. The label even controls where we *put* every part that we're handling. It pinpoints the very spot in the facility where that part will be placed as it awaits shipment. If the part is special ordered for a particular car owner, the location for the dealer and the customer's name and phone number will be printed on the label. When it arrives at the dealership, the counter person knows who to call to notify them that their part has arrived. Every key piece of information is tacked onto that part for its entire ride through the distribution system. (Don't you wish that we could get that kind of information accountability for every dollar that each of us pays in taxes?)

From 10,000 to 12,000 lines per day are shipped out. The label allows us to pick multiple dealers at once. *We ship every in-stock item that has been ordered the day it has been ordered.* If a dealer orders it by 11 AM, it's shipped that day and received by the dealer the next day. You can imagine what that does for customer satisfaction at the dealer level. Between 15 and 18 truckloads travel out each day. Off to the side of the dock, you can see the traffic manager's office. The Phantom Traffic Manager. Its glass-walled interior is dark, the walls are empty and the door has been closed for four years. I guess that our distribution department keeps it around for the sake of nostalgia. That vacant office is a real achievement. The *label* is our TRAFFIC MANAGER today because data on the label generates all the necessary bills of lading.

Our accuracy goal is one in 1,400. In 1993, we improved to one error in 2,700 for the first time. We've had months where we've run this business with one in 4,000. When the rare error is made, we not only are able to tell the person that they made a mistake—as most quality control systems do—we are also able to tell them *what mistake they made.* Most mistakes follow a pattern, and we track those too. Is Dick or Debbie picking high, picking low...to the side? Our Associate turnover is so low because people get better and better through constructive coaching, and the focus of that coaching is patterns of behavior rather than pointing to individual incidents with no information on what exactly went wrong.

Bob Arnett has been with us more than 20 years and his on-top-of-everything right-hand people—George Shepard and Ray Grillo—make sure that the operation is completely organized: the time of day certain items are picked, and the specific bin where a particular part is located (the computer assigns the part's home, of course). On the foundation that Bob France built, Bob Arnett skillfully extended the parts department, making it even more efficient. Bob Arnett saw the information-technology potential in parts management and put great stress on devising an information-packed label we put on each parts order and made the label the tool to carry information. After all, if the label could carry the load rather than people, we would be so much further ahead. And that is exactly what Bob and his team achieved. We have the ability today to use optical scanners to read the labels, and some day we may—if the process were to prove cost effective. But, today it doesn't seem necessary because an Associate will know that the home of a particular 12-digit part code is the third aisle up on the top shelf.

We are trying to duplicate the physical look of corresponding parts facilities in Japan, so that Associates on both sides of the ocean have the same "mental map" of a parts distribution center. That's not to say that all of our parts come from Japan. Three hundred to three hundred fifty containers (not always full ones) are domestically sourced. These are genuine Toyota parts made by domestic American vendors in synch with Toyota's own domestic sourcing goals in the United States. These are parts that go into the assembly-line products in Toyota's Kentucky and California NUMMI plants as well and must be of perfect quality.

Housekeeping that would pass muster in the Marines and a passion for safety have been trademarks of the present Jacksonville Parts Distribution Center since it opened in 1978. We have banners hanging down that recognize our Safety and Housekeeping Award Program. We have had no lost-time injuries in the past four years. A big reason, I think, is that our Associates inspect their own areas for potential safety concerns. The Center's communications hub has five laser printers. The operator can't go home until the last order is filled, shipped, and billed. The last act of the evening is a computer handshake that certifies all the requested parts are shipped. And, then, lights out. As usual, it's been another active and productive day in Jacksonville.

But, you know what I like best of all about our Jacksonville Parts operation? *The roller skates!* Several of the aisles where none of the power equipment is permitted are stocked with thousands of the tiniest parts, including washers. On a strictly voluntary basis, Associates there are permitted to rollerskate as they collect parts for shipping. They love it, and *it works!*

Red wagons to roller skates. Maybe we haven't come so far after all. But there's a secret ingredient in the middle: I put that wagon into motion selling pop on the basis of intuition. The roller skates go into action based on specific hard data. And where does the data come from? You guessed it...the computer. If I hadn't been lucky enough to believe in the importance of two marvels of 20th-century technology, I might still be eking out a living on a Chicago used-car lot. The first was TELEVISION...and the second was the COMPUTER.

"Even back in 1969, Jim Moran knew that the flow of information between the distributor and the dealer had to be clear and concise. In one sense or another, all products flow down that information highway. As the quality of information goes, so goes the business."

—Ed Machek
President,
Information Technology Services

I've always believed in the importance of information. Information is the pulse. Many entrepreneurs—especially of my generation—resist or once resisted data processing. I didn't see how you could. Early in 1969, we put old 33 ASR teletypes with paper tape out in the field. We would poll the dealers every night for car sales, trades, and parts orders. This became our pipeline. These chattering machines were primitive, but they gave us the first computerized information network in an automobile distributorship. At headquarters, all we had were punch-tape records with sales and parts orders. Nonetheless, that was Star-Wars sophistication back in 1969. Every morning, we knew immediately if there was a fall-off in sales or if the consumer's color-scheme preference was shifting.

We still do. We are in a revolution, revving up the next generation of computer power. Since 1984, the real tide in computers has turned. It's not getting *more* data, but being able to *use* the data that you already have well. Our World Omni subsidiary in Mobile has become a finance-industry showcase for advanced technology. They have already cut five million files down to three million. These are being digitized (the newest and most compact form of computer record keeping) and stored on compact disks. One of the Kodak scanners we use can digitize 120 pieces of paper a minute. If the paper is folded or crumpled, it will even unfold it or straighten it out!

It was Ed Machek who really put us on the map as far as computers were concerned. Ed hailed from Chicago as I did and joined our team as one of our original Associates back in 1969. He built our data processing program from scratch into an entire division now called Information Technology Services. Ed Machek says that cars today are on "information tracks" from the day they're born, just like a ride at Disneyworld, with nothing neglected or left to chance. He's right. We know the whole history. When it was built, shipped, arrived at port, wholesaled to the dealer, and retailed to the consumer. With history like that, is it any wonder that Toyota is constantly able to build a better car?

Each dealership now has the data processing power we had centrally just a few years ago. To do the job at the distributor level, I was unwilling to forego the information quality that I had as a dealer. That's how you make it easier for a dealership today.

"Toyota went to school on Jim Moran. He is the 'dealer's dealer,' and his pioneer work allowed us to move so many concepts—from Toyotathons to a finance company—further upstream in our own thinking."

> — Jim Press
> Senior Vice President
> and General Manager,
> TMS USA, Inc.
> Lexus Division

We were the first ones to automate bill-of-sale invoices and certificates of origin. For years, other car distributors had teams of typists working just so that the dealerships could sell cars. For a long time, we have had forms popping off the machine in seconds. Our own automation as a distributor really made our dealers more ready to accept computerization and automation within their own businesses. If you want to be believed and accepted, you must lead by example.

"Why did we take on Toyota? Very frankly, we figured if it was good enough for Jim Moran it was good enough for us."

—Jerry Bean
Owner and President,
Kendall Toyota (America's
largest Toyota dealership)

The computer plays a crucial role in our car allocations. In the allocation system, we've been very observant of market demands and needs. Putting the cars in the right place has been a major information-systems priority. Unlike most distributors who have cars sitting at the port for a month or two or are even celebrating *birthdays* there, ours are pre-allocated on the ship crossing. Dealers know what cars are coming when the cars are at sea. Allocation systems are fundamentally driven by fixed rules that analyze sales trends to distribute the product fairly. But the earlier you give the dealer information on the product they will be getting, the earlier that they can fine-tune their selling plan. It even allows us to re-distribute some of the units before they land to accommodate dealers who may want to trade between themselves.

It makes a great big difference for a dealer to know what specific cars he'll have in 10 days to two weeks, because the dealer is then in a position to "sell" the allocations under way. It's like having a factory on the water. Delays are minimal. On average, cars move through the port in two to three days.

Another subject that we continue to study very carefully is the customer. That's true for us, and it's true for Toyota too. Before they sign off on a new product concept, Toyota City will send in a study team of eight to twelve people for ten to fifteen days to Southeast Toyota asking questions and simply observing. For example, we recommended one of Toyota's teams watch customers at a local Publix supermarket in Florida. What in the world could a car maker hope to learn from watching how customers behave at a supermarket? In a word: Groceries. Where do shoppers put their groceries? Do they set them on the front seat or on the front floor, the back seat or the back floor, or maybe in the trunk? What is going to make it most convenient for shopping? How does the storage choice vary by size of grocery purchase or if kids are along for the ride? What size and bulk of grocery purchases are most common? Everybody knows that the family car is often a grocery van, but how often and in what ways? If you aren't expert about how people store groceries, you can't design a truly functional car.

Toyota's management keeps asking us to help arrange lifestyle studies. We started to help Toyota with the study that led to the 1994 Camry back in 1990. It might sound fancy, but it's nothing much more than intelligent "people-watching". We will park the team in front of a delicatessen in a neighborhood with older people and point out other cars in the new targeted size range, focusing on the features that probably made those cars appealing to their owners: larger interior space, the width of the door opening, and a full-sized spare instead of a donut.[23] These features all spell convenience and ease of movement. Handling characteristics are important too: The car should be *sturdy and roomy*—but not so big that it is difficult to drive. Older consumers don't usually like vibrant colors. Most prefer more sedate, cooler shades and iridescent lacquers.

---

[23] I just want any seniors reading this book to know that I continue to campaign for *bench seats* versus bucket seats as an option for the models that are most popular with you.

A few weeks before every trip I make to Japan, I start to stir the coals and ask people to raise issues about how we can influence the *current* product ideas coming out of Japan. Toyota doesn't make many mistakes, but they will always make a bad marketing decision before they even consider making a bad quality decision. And is that ever the right attitude!

There is no more important grassroots input than what we learn from our dealers. When a distribution manager orders a month's production of vehicles, he or she is making a $140- to $150-million commitment. No distributor can afford to have such a check drawn based on one person's judgment. No matter what a genius that person may be, you can't know the marketplace as quickly as it can change.

You need the sales-floor experience of what sold last month and why. Huge commitments only work through partnerships. We actually go out to the dealers and go through our physical production order line-by-line and ask them to challenge the order that we're intending to submit. By model, we ask them to step through the color spread to tell us what trends they are noticing. One hundred percent South Florida input won't, of course, satisfy the needs of Muscle Shoals, Alabama. It's a totally new kind of specification purchasing. SET constantly fine-tunes decisions. We have to be *right* now for deliveries three or four months from now, anticipating what the factories will be building then.

"We Associates have a strong sense of ownership in what happens here. We like operating in overdrive. The culture and the ésprits-de-corps of the Associates feeds on itself."

> — *Casey Gunnell*
> *Executive Vice President*
> *Chief Financial Officer,*
> *JM Family*

That's a glimpse of what you might call mega-tech marketing. It's exciting, modernistic, and—most of all—it works. But, the reason it works is that we have such skilled and committed Associates and Dealers putting it into practice.

Jim Moran: In Appreciation

I started doing business with Jim's companies in about 1974. I guess I was lucky that he was doing business in the area in which I began my business. His companies were always creative, energetic and, most of all, willing to take a chance on somebody starting out. Really, he and one other great auto person, Ed Morse, were key figures in the success of Alamo Rent A Car.

I began to know Jim personally much later than I began doing business with him. We actually became acquainted through Ed Morse and through the numerous charities which we both support. When I got to know Jim and Jan, I realized he was a warm and caring person and always had a business idea or two to talk over which made it lots of fun to be with him.

Jim is one of those unique Americans who underscore "The American Story". That is: If you've got the energy, if you dream the dream, if you put your nose to the grindstone, if you bring value to your customers and have a little bit of style, America is the most fertile ground for a person to make it in the world. Jim is truly a man who proves this theory over and over.

—*Michael Egan*
Chairman
Alamo Rent A Car

Of all the people I mention in this book, the one person whom I haven't talked about much so far is my wife, Jan. She is soft-spoken and supportive. But she influences many things in a positive way behind the scenes. We have a real pact on health matters because of all the problems I've gone through. I might crave a Snickers or a tenderloin steak, but she keeps me on the low cholesterol, low fat straight-and-narrow. In JM Family Enterprises, Jan is a senior vice president who runs our marine fleet and extensive aircraft operations. She does a superlative job! If you ever visit the hangar for our jets, you'd swear that the spotless polyurethane-coated floor was covered with a sheet of glass. Her ideas are evident in the design and appointments of our ships and planes...and in our award-winning Deerfield Beach offices, designed by master architect Bob Broward (who studied under Frank Lloyd Wright) and that opened in 1981. We wanted a headquarters with a quiet face and backdrop to a high-energy pace. She gave us that touch. As visitors have told me, shouting seems absolutely out of place there. Most of all, I remember her support at the rough times, like the 15 days and nights that she spent next to me on a cot in the hospital as I recovered from open-heart surgery. Jan is a most caring and loving person.

It's dusk now on the *Gallant Lady*, and we have just witnessed the elusive green flash over the ocean in the Bahamas as the sun sizzles below the horizon like a firey emerald. We've talked enough about *making it*, and I've just about run out of ideas on what let me become successful. Let's talk about some things that are even more important: What you do with your success if you're lucky enough to attain it...and how we might all think about building a better country.

TELL IT LIKE IT IS

"Giving Back May Be the Best Part of Getting" by Rabbi Merle E. Singer

There are few—if any—people I know who get more personal satisfaction from giving than Jim Moran does. Whether it's rewarding his Associates at year-end or tipping an extra few dollars to a young waiter from Haiti just starting out in our country, you can just see the gleam in his eye as he practices what he calls "giving back." Particularly when worthy charities are involved, sometimes the giving reaches epic proportions. One time a volunteer solicitor came in to his office hoping for a modest donation to Miami Children's Hospital and walked out with a commitment for $100,000! He is truly a man of vision who has made the difference in literally hundreds of thousands of lives.

Jim is very reluctant to talk about his contributions. A sizable portion are made anonymously. He may mention his involvement with the Youth Automotive Training Center because he would like more individuals and firms to play a role in that cause and its potential expansion. Jim might describe how the folks at Courtesy Ford rallied in support after the devastating Our Lady of the Angels school fire because he was proud of their community spirit...just as he might comment with pride on how Pat Moran spearheaded an effort to drop holiday-season gift giving in the corporate headquarters. Instead Associates now channel the money to local charities, last year giving over $47,000 for the holiday period alone. Jim Moran and charity, gracious giving, are synonymous!

Many people believe that the longest, deepest tradition of business giving is to be found in the American Midwest. Maybe that's true because of the spirit of community cooperation that has its roots in the pioneer days as the great prairies were settled. Jim's energy and sheer volume of campaigns that he organized during his days in Chicago are subjects of awe in the business circles of the Windy City. Jim Moran brought that giving with him when he moved to Florida. He became an early supporter of the auto industry's Northwood University when it established an outreach campus in Florida from its base in Michigan. They conferred on him a prestigious Doctor of Laws degree in 1987.

Jim is generous to a fault in his giving and not haphazard. He is tough-minded about investing donations where they will do the most good. One example includes Jim and Jan Moran's gift of half a million dollars to the Broward Community Foundation (which was matched by other donors as part of a challenge grant) to benefit disadvantaged youth and to help them make the most of work and educational opportunities.

What Jim does is not just philanthropy because philanthropy means love of man...You only give philanthropy out of love for humankind. It is not charity because charity is based in *caritas*, which is to hold dear, or to love. You give alms only when you feel for people. What Jim Moran does goes beyond all of this and is described in the Hebrew word *tzedakah*—righteousness— "it doesn't make any difference how you feel; it is right, it is just, to give to others." The highest form of *tzedakah*—righteous giving—is giving someone a chance to learn how to take care of themselves, to learn a trade, to gain the confidence to provide for themselves and others...and that is what Jim does best.

When they've been surveyed, JM Family Associates have told Jim that their top interest in charitable giving and volunteer interests is education. Activities to benefit at-risk youth are second and the environment is third. More than 70 percent of the JM Family staff are or have been involved in volunteer work in the community. This is a tribute to Jim Moran's ideals and principles. His staff resemble him in their style: soft-spoken extroverts, with determination and a genuine belief that they have an obligation to serve the community.

In addition to his many on-going charitable endeavors, when there is a crisis in the region you can count on Jim being there, too, and usually in person. When Jamaica had a hurricane several years ago, the company's jets sped medical relief and supplies there. When Hurricane Andrew hit Florida in 1992, the jets once again conveyed supplies to hurricane-ravaged sites, and ground vehicles were dedicated to disaster work. Tons of crucially needed ice were trucked in and given away free. JM Family Enterprises made an additional donation of $150,000 to the Broward Community Foundation.

This kind of giving is happening quietly and constantly. It may not be the most self-serving public relations but it's in keeping with a philosophy that Jim and his organization believe in...if you do something nice, make sure people don't feel indebted to you for it.

Some Concluding Thoughts

Watching kids work on cars still gives me a good feeling. I'm sure it takes me back to my days as a young-ster...but I think it's more than that. Being a skilled mechanic is as worthwhile a trade today as it was 50 years ago. It may take less muscle power to lift heavy parts in the 1990s, but the computer diagnostic equipment and the space-age electronics of today's autos also demand a lot more mental concentration.

In 1984, the Youth Automotive Training Center (YATC) in Hollywood, Florida, was opened. Over the years, like most businesses, we've backed quite a few social programs and have felt it was the right thing to do. When you've had some good fortune, you give back to help those less fortunate. Of all the programs, this one has been the most satisfying. YATC is a school for special kids—at-risk, disadvantaged youth from southern Florida between the ages of 16 and 21. The school teaches these boys and girls the basics of auto mechanics. There are five people on the faculty. We enroll 20 students each year. Our graduation success rate is 75-80 percent. Annually we award several scholarships for further study to the best qualified Center graduates. Additional support for YATC comes off the fairways. For the past eight years, we've had a golf classic—last year at Grand Cypress in Orlando—to raise money for the school. Last year, 625 people attended that event; and we raised over $330,000 in net proceeds. Our tournament includes a $50,000 hole-in-one. Three years ago we had a winner.[24] And I'm glad we did because it couldn't have stirred interest in a better cause.

> *"When I attended my first YATC graduation, the strongest impression it made on me was that Jim Moran wasn't just there to contribute financially. He was there to give of himself—of his very being—to inspire others to achieve their own goals."*
>
> — *Judge Melanie May*
> *Broward County Juvenile Court Judge*

Students are referred by social agencies, churches, and the judicial system; but word-of-mouth from people active in the community is our biggest source. Their personal backgrounds are generally troubled and may involve drug or alcohol abuse, poverty, dysfunctional families, and/or homelessness.

The nine-month class covers the complete car bumper to bumper, with a balanced diet of classroom learning and garage reality, starting with textbook training in the morning. We keep the large library totally up to date. IBM chipped in with computers and with free training. We have academic staff to help the kids get their GED—the equivalent of a high-school diploma. The afternoon is hands-on in the shop—the only way to go for mechanical skills. So many vocational schools train with obsolete equipment and

---

[24] Fortunately we were playing by U.S. rules rather than Japanese ones because in the United States the price of success may only be a round of drinks. In Japan, if somebody lands a hole-in-one they have to buy their golfing comrades expensive commemorative gifts. The "good luck" is in fact so costly that many Japanese actually buy "hole-in-one" insurance to protect themselves from such a "lucky" shock wave hitting their wallet.°

graduate kids with out-of-date skills. The technology at YATC is state-of-the-art. We have the latest machinery, including front end alignment gear, a modern valve grinder and a computerized scope. Not long ago, we added a six-dome outdoor extension that doubles our training space. The addition was funded by our golf tournament.

We learned that we can't just teach the brains and the hands. Often you have to help the soul and the will too. After six hours of clean, positive learning; what should the student go back to? We learned soon enough what the other reality most faced was like: 18 hours a day scraping by to survive and living in a bad home life. If you want young people to turn around, you have to do more. That's why we provide counseling and other help. But social theory is blue sky. Let me give you some real cases.

"It's here or nowhere."
"If it wasn't for this school, I'd be in prison right now."

—YATC Students

I'll call this young man "Jack". He is a husky 6'3" and a good 230 pounds today. Thin as a railbird when he joined us, he came from a home with a negligent mom. Jack was rubber-stamped "incorrigible"—looking for trouble and threading his way through more than five foster homes between the ages of 13 and 16. He was displaced, angry, rebellious, and down-and-out by the time he applied to us. A foster mother told him that he better latch on to something like YATC or life was going to be a grim one-way street.

The issue is teaching self-discipline.

"The most important thing is to be a star in your own mind. That's how these kids feel when they come out of YATC...This community should be very grateful that we have people like Jim Moran who have given us this program."

—Judge Robert Collins
Administrative Juvenile Division,
Broward County

Did he have a knack for cars! Jack could jury-rig any-thing. He really turned around when we took him out of his runaway shelter "home" and helped subsidize his housing, food, and transportation. Knowing that people cared and having that basic support, he got the confidence to believe that he could do it on his own. Without the counseling and an economic start-up, forget the vo-tech training. It rarely works by itself.

Here's a kid who was living in a car, homeless, and with-out a dime to his name, who now travels through the state of Florida with a responsible job for a towing company. He has his own address and two children and takes care of the mother of those children and the boys. If YATC or some-thing like it hadn't intervened, where do you think that he would be?

> *"Jim Moran is a special person (in the way he thinks and acts on behalf of children)...I think that the success or failure of a young person rests on the shoulders of an adult...Society makes kids, and society breaks them..."*
>
> — *Chi Chi Rodriguez*
> *PGA Golf Champion*

William Borraiz was born in Bogota, Colombia, in 1966. He has dark brown eyes, a wide smile, and a sturdy build that comes from his avid devotion to bicycle racing. The people at YATC describe William with two phrases—"incredibly motivated" and "appreciative". Here's a young man who pulled himself up from tough economic conditions and managed a perfect attendance record. Today, he works at Sears doing front-end alignment and suspension. One day he has the goal of going back to his native Colombia and help-ing out economically disadvantaged people there. And, you know, I bet he will.

Many kids in the program come from indigent fami-lies. So our first private-life emphasis is food, clothing, and transportation. We fix their cars. We put the mother or father in a job-training program, but we don't provide dollars to the families directly. We may try to help the student with a little financial boost. Last week, I was thumbing through the alumni records. Same pattern, again and again: drug rehab, time in a correctional institution or foster home...alternating with sweeping floors or the lowest rungs as a temporary worker.

Fall 1994 marked the tenth anniversary of YATC. Bill Cosby joined us to help celebrate the event and gave a special performance for the school at the Sunrise Musical Theatre in Sunrise, Florida. That visit and other fundraisers celebrating YATC's first decade were festive. But, the most rewarding part of the celebration was recognition for the great success the program has had in turning around young lives. The sold-out banquet (one of the best managed business events I've ever witnessed) brought in hundreds of business leaders from throughout the region. Former New York Governor Hugh Carey, J. P. Bolduc (one of the finest business executives I know), and John Sununu, former White House chief of staff, helped spread the YATC story and raise awareness to a totally new level. Many students have come to us because they were fascinated by cars, but the auto service skills...important as they may be...are often a pathway to something far more important: a stable, productive personal life with a stronger basic education and clearer life goals.

"During the last thirty years of my professional career as a teacher, lawyer, and judge, I have come to know three men who are giants in the field of helping children at risk. They're Jim Casey, the founder of United Parcel Service... Jack Eckerd, the founder of Eckerd Drugstores... and Jim Moran..."

—Judge Frank Orlando
Retired Circuit Court and
Juvenile Court Judge

One of our finest YATC alumni is someone I'll call "Terrence". Today he has determination and self-confidence, but it wasn't always that way. Terrence was the product of a broken home and lived with his dad, until his father passed away in 1986. Never one for book learning, he scarcely dreamed of going to college. One of his teachers was so negative he told the class, "I hope I have you again, so I can fail you again." While he had some excellent and committed teachers, Terrence's experience in the public-school system paralleled what has happened to so many other African-American young people.

Terrence's life became aimless, and he didn't hit his stride again until YATC restored his faith in himself and his abilities. He was always good at tinkering with things, but YATC gave him the chance to master some of the other rudiments of learning at the right pace. After he graduated, Terrence went on to college. Today he's a video technician at a progressive electronics manufacturer and an entrepreneur, too—with a photography and auto-stereo installation business in his off hours. Without the YATC background, he says today, he'd still probably be washing cars. Now, he's married and thinking his future out with a seriousness anybody would admire, and he seeks out chances to tell other kids with similar backgrounds *they* can make it too!

Sounds heart-warming, and it often is. Especially at the holidays, I try to spend some time with the kids, and it's great to hear from them that our caring has given them a glimpse of hope. But there's a tough side to backing a program like this: The choosing. We start with dozens of referrals, narrow the list to 35, and finally reduce the entry class to 20. In the midst of this, we hear the stories. Homeless. Mother has cancer. During one board meeting as we were in the middle of a kid's profile, I threw up my hands and said that I just don't know how these people do it. I think of myself as fairly street-smart; and I've known some tough times, but the desperate jungle many of our young people live in is unbelievable.

"In the 15 years I have known Jim Moran, I have never seen him as youthful or as vibrant as when he is dealing with the kids at YATC. That program and its students have given a whole new dimension to his life—and he obviously loves it."

— Ray Bergan
Williams & Connolly

Maybe someday there will be more slots at YATC. Maybe someday there will be more programs like YATC. I hope it happens and that other firms and individuals step up and start programs like this. And I hope for something more and different, too. I hope that we can muster the guts to change attitudes toward work and responsibility in our country.

The future can only begin with kids and some of our family will be carrying forward the Moran tradition. The one who is really on the firing line today is Pat. I remember when Pat used to come to my office and dust the shelves and desk. She couldn't even have been 10 years old, and she would poke around the papers and ask endless questions. Even then, she was curious about the business. And she really understood the idea of turning a family business into a business family at a pretty early age. I have to catch myself these days because I don't want to sound paternalistic, but I still say to her: "Now, Pat, we have a lot of family to take care of." It still slips out, and I guess that's the way I really feel down deep, and it will never change.

Today, Pat is a mature and poised business woman. As President, Pat has come along fast and done a sensational job. She's learned much from managers like Jim Press. I think that she'll always do a good job because she likes people and she likes to work. She likes what she's doing and knows that she must surround herself with good people. Most of all, she has staying power and determination. When the wind blows against Pat, she'll reverse it. And she's bringing along a whole new generation of managers—like John Williams—to make sure that we stay ahead of the challenges.

I single out John because he is a completely home-grown talent and because of the especially high regard in which he is held by our dealers.

Not long ago, Pat summed up the transition we have gone through pretty eloquently—I thought—in some comments she developed for a management meeting. I'm including them below because I think that they do such a good job of describing where we've been and where we're going:

> We can never forget that Toyota made us. We didn't make them. Jim Moran has said that countless times, and I believe it every bit as much as he does.
>
> All of us—the distributorship and dealers alike—have prospered as the business has grown dramatically. But the business has also changed in a very fundamental way from being strictly retail to being intensely customer-service driven today.
>
> For SET, that has meant equipping ourselves with the people and the technology to listen better to our dealers...so that they could be more professional in caring for the retail customer.
>
> The role of SET management is that of integrator and coordinator—more focused on sensing and defining direction than in giving direction in any heavy-handed way. Among the SET staff, we have placed a real priority on transplanting the "owner" mentality throughout the rest of the team in all of our companies. But it is all for just one end: The most important duty that we as support staff have is to constantly be out listening to what our dealers in the field have to say and to act on that input.

There's a special philosophy that has guided me over the years, and I know that it steers Pat and all our Associates in just about everything that we do. We call it the philosophy of "The Three C's": *Consideration, cooperation, communication*. Toyota's Shotaro Kamiya, the founder of Toyota Motor Sales and Yukiyasu Togo, recently retired Chairman of Toyota Motor Sales, USA, really taught me that philosophy, and

I'm forever indebted to them for it. If anything, I've just condensed and interpreted it. But I think that it's the soundest, most durable advice for running a business that I've ever learned; and I'm brash enough to recommend it to the rest of American business as the right track to take.

I personally think there is a lot we can learn from the Japanese. In his classic study of international competition, Dean Lester Thurow of MIT's Sloan School of Management points out: "Studies of automation show that when automation goes up in America, wages go down. In contrast, when automation rises in Japan, wages rise. In Japan these investments are used to enhance the productivity of labor rather than to replace skilled labor with unskilled labor, as happens in the United States."[P] Too often, we imitate Japanese management practices but do it in a superficial way—going for the short-term gain and forgetting the more important long-term purpose they were originally designed to serve by the Japanese when they shaped these ideas.

A few years back, Sony's then CEO Akio Morita and Shintaro Ishihara wrote a book that was published in Japan, called *The Japan That Can Say 'No'*. It contended that Japan had come of age and really didn't have to live in the shadow of the West and especially of America any more. Nobody disputes that. But I think that the really constructive message for America is *not* the Japan that can say no, but the America that can say *yes*—and learn a few things from the Japanese success story:

to say yes to higher educational standards, and education that is really practical and relevant...

to say yes to absolutely the toughest standards of quality...

to say yes to sensible collaboration between government and industry, like Japan's MITI endorses, that can make us better competitors abroad...

to say yes to loyalty within our companies—instead of having management and workers be adversaries...

I learned a long time ago that the power of thinking YES beats the power of thinking NO any day of the week. If

you talk to the brightest people in the American auto industry, they will tell you—maybe not when the tape recorder
or video camera is running, but they will tell you in private—
that Japan may be the best thing that ever happened to Detroit. It taught the domestic auto industry that it must build
quality cars to survive. And I'm not even sure that you can
call a company like Toyota—which has more than fifteen
billion dollars invested in the United States, directly employs 16,000 workers and indirectly employs another 68,000
in dealerships, and exports 43,000 U.S.-built cars each
year—a Japanese company in the strict sense of the word.
It's a global business, and reality today is truly global, too.

　　Take it from the "pop boy" on the baseball diamonds
behind Senn High, saying YES to positive, fresh, energizing
ideas and persisting in a steady, low-key way can take you a
long way in this life.

Afterword

Dr. Melvin Stith
Dean, Florida State University College of Business

Flowers. Cards. A brief, encouraging phone call nearly every day. That's what I remember most sitting by my wife Pat's bedside as she recovered from surgery for breast cancer two years ago. These kind greetings came from our caring friends Jim and Jan Moran. Jim himself knew the leveling effect of cancer. He almost succumbed to it more than a quarter-century ago. And, when friends or acquaintances in the community face that life-threatening disease, Jim makes it a special point to stay in touch. I think he knows how much constant, low-key contact encourages and sustains a positive outlook as the cancer patient and the patient's family go through the challenge of recovery. I'm pleased to say that Pat *has* recovered and is back on the job today as a department head in the university community and as a mother of three children.

My wife made a great comeback, and Jim Moran has been a great role model for us. He has done a remarkable job in coming back from adversity during his life. When Jim talks about selling pop out of a wagon on Chicago's North Side as a youngster, it's a childhood experience I can relate to with ease. As a kid, I picked cotton, and I worked my way through college as a restaurant cook in Philadelphia during the summers.

When I left the marketing department at Florida A&M University to join the faculty at FSU and ultimately become dean of its Business School in July 1991, I too had come a long way. Rather than the tough streets of Chicago, my journey was from the family farm in Jarratt, Virginia, near the North Carolina border. My parents never had the opportunity to go to high school, but all nine of my brothers and sisters went to college. In fact, all of them received degrees.

We would never have gotten anywhere without the love and encouragement of our parents. Jim appreciates the value of parents. Since his Dad died when Jim was still so young, Jim's mother played an important role in developing and fostering his values—especially his integrity, his industriousness and his high regard for people. His mother, Anna Moran must have been a remarkable woman; and he, his mother, and his sister struggled against some pretty tough times during the Depression in Chicago.

Being poor is another kind of leveling effect, different from cancer, but often drastic, too. Jim Moran understands the meaning of being poor. In truly caring people, knowing the struggle to survive first-hand and knowing it early in life establishes a remarkable kinship with others. That's why giving back means so much to Jim. Giving back doesn't translate to mere dollars. For him, it means opportunity, a chance at self-realization.

Some very special people will be graduating college and getting advanced degrees at Florida State University as the result of Jim Moran's generosity. That means a lot to me personally, and I also learned why making education possible for young people meant so much to Jim Moran through my membership on the board of directors of YATC, an organization Jim describes so well in his closing comments to this book. I've been fortunate to serve on the board of YATC since 1992 and have witnessed so many breakthroughs in young lives become realities through this ambitious program. Florida State scholarships for both YATC graduates and winners of African-American Achiever Awards will be a very important part of the Jim Moran Institute for Global Entrepreneurship which has been created at Florida State University. I'll tell you more about the Entrepreneurship program in just a moment, but let me first describe the African-American Achiever Awards.

JM Family and Southeast Toyota Distributors presented their first annual African-American Achiever Awards in 1993. I felt then as I do now that the Achiever Awards are a logical extension of what YATC does for minorities and the disadvantaged. The community in south Florida (Dade, Broward, and Palm Beach Counties) is invited to identify nominees for the Awards during February—when Black History Month is celebrated each year. Honorees are then picked by an independent panel of distinguished African-American community leaders. The selection of the winners is publicized, they are honored at a dinner reception, and a grant is made on their behalf to the charity or community organization of their choice.

These Awards help create role models, and one of the nicest features is that Award recipients are picked from eight different categories for personal achievement: the arts, business, community involvement, education, government, health and family services, non-profit organizations, and the professions. Youngsters are given a wide range of role models—mentors who will match their personal interests and aspirations.

Award winners in the past several years have included some pretty remarkable people, and I'll mention just a few of them:

State Representative Beryl D. Burke, for example, was elected to the Florida House of Representatives in 1992, and the Miami Herald *named her the most effective of Dade County's freshman legislators.*

Fort Lauderdale attorney Charles W. Cherry II, in addition to being a lawyer, has written a book titled Excellence Without Excuse: The Black Student's Guide to Academic Excellence *and frequently talks to student groups about how to improve academic skills.*

Georgia Foster founded a Miami-based organization called Think Life, Inc., that provides housing for HIV/AIDS victims and their families. Its annual budget is now $500,000 with 25 families served.

Metro-Dade Police Chief Jimmie Brown was honored for his outstanding community involvement and his exceptional career achievements.

In 1996, I'm delighted to report that the program will be expanded to confer awards to African-American youths as well as adults. Deborah Work wrote a memorable column in the *Fort Lauderdale Sun Sentinel*[q] following a conversation she had with Jim after JM Family's most recent African-American Achiever Awards Program. She transmitted—I felt—the depth and sincerity of Jim Moran's understanding of our country's racial turmoil in the past. Leaders like Jim Moran are committed to more than understanding. They genuinely want to bring about a stronger, sounder foundation and that means a focus on children.

The African-American Achiever Awards were Step Two in my opinion. Step Three was the establishment of the Jim Moran Institute for Global Entrepreneurship. The Institute was set up in June 1995 with a one-million dollar grant from Jim Moran with a matching $750,000 grant from the state of Florida. While not intended to benefit minorities and the disadvantaged exclusively, certain aspects of the program—which is extraordinarily comprehensive in scope—are earmarked for that express purpose.

Why does all this matter? Some statistics will demonstrate the importance of small business entrepreneurship to our nation's economy and competitiveness...and why doing something to further entrepreneurship is so important right now.

- First of all, it's a matter of jobs. Ninety-eight percent of the firms in America have a hundred employees or fewer, and the trend toward smaller companies is continuing.
- In fact, small companies are four times more likely to create jobs than large, multinational businesses.
- While small businesses are crucial to job growth within our country and to our economic competitiveness abroad, these companies are fragile—especially when they try to grow into medium- and larger-sized companies. A recent *Business Week* article points out, "Small companies typically see growth rates slow as they get bigger—while investors tend to bail out at the first sign results are weakening and move money into companies earlier in the growth cycle."[r]

The truth is that small-business entrepreneurs *are* disadvantaged, and there are few people who understand the plight of the disadvantaged of all sorts better than Jim Moran. The small business founder or operator today has never been expected to master so much basic business knowledge and yet to be a pioneer and develop new ideas and applications besides.

Jim Moran has found his niche in the world of education. Jim is a natural teacher, by the way, and a born educator. This became apparent when he first visited our campus in Tallahassee in 1995, and it didn't surprise me since a talent for teaching is sometimes strongest in people without considerable formal education. While he had been on a college campus to receive an honorary degree before, he had never been in a university classroom setting in his life. He immediately "connected" with the faculty, students and business entrepreneurs who had been invited to the event. He laid out his plan with such clarity of insight. If I and the School of Business faculty are convinced of one thing, it is that this endowment is both a powerful challenge as well as a vote of confidence. Faculty members have told me that this must be the beginning of something much bigger, not an end in itself—a conviction I, of course, share.

Why was Florida State picked for this program? Maybe one reason is that we have a large undergraduate program in business, while a number of other universities tend to make business a post-graduate study. We think our approach has some merits because so many skills—from problem-solving to information technology and systems—would be better mastered earlier in a student's life. It was Jim's wife Jan and JM Family Enterprises Executive Vice President Wayne McClain who really encouraged the development of the FSU program. As excellent sounding boards for Jim Moran, they knew that Jim really wanted to make a large-scale grant to education, but he also wanted that investment to be different from the typical business-school endowment that too often encourages elitism and scholarly formality. Instead he wanted a program that would be accessible, focused on applied learning. Above all, he wanted an educational mindset characterized by loyalty, compassion, and caring.

What goes into the program? I won't even go into detail about the Jim Moran Lecture Hall or the Entrepreneur of the Year Awards that will be granted—although both of these facets of the program are deeply appreciated. Some of the other key aspects include the following:

- Four professorships will be established, and one of these professors will become the Director of the Jim Moran Institute of Global Entrepreneurship. These professorships are extremely important to the future of the Florida State School of Business because we—

like so many other state business schools—are prone to lose some of our brightest young faculty members to schools with a tad more prestige. The professors as a group will provide teaching, research, and service to the Institute.

- Scholarships to Florida State for YATC graduates are a key part of the program as is scholarship support for recipients of African-American Achiever Youth Awards, beginning in 1996.
- Annually the Institute will sponsor a one-day Conference on Global Entrepreneurship that will help small business owners become more efficient and effective in what they do. The Conference will help businesses discuss and solve routine problems. We are committed to keep the conferences pragmatic and multi-focused, so that we are as likely to deal with the challenges facing a local dry cleaning or restaurant chain as we are to address the agenda of an advanced software firm or manufacturer of high-tech ceramics. We especially want to get vendors to small businesses involved so owners of emerging firms understand the needs and framework of the businesses that serve them.

We want the annual Conference to become the cornerstone for a year-round *style* of communications that will involve students, faculty members, and entrepreneurs in the community as they learn about and help solve the actual problems and answer the information needs of small businesses. We also want to create a powerful regional network, built around the solution of "real-live" problems and the realization of concrete opportunities. After I thought about Jim's vision for the program for several weeks, I saw the real genius it contained. Here was a fresh vision for business education modeled on the kind of success Jim and his people have achieved at Southeast Toyota and JM Family. He was projecting the network and systems that had worked so well in solving business problems into the world of education.

That's the highest level of communication that can take place in the business academic world!

Jim has made it clear that the program is in no sense designed to promote or benefit sectors of the auto industry. The whole spectrum of industries will benefit, but this grant will—I believe—be particularly important to fostering entrepreneurship in our state's all-important service sectors.

Jim has always been on the edge of the future. He just has a sense for it. Maybe that's part of the wonder of how his heart and mind work. It's beyond definition. It was true with Jim and television marketing, and it's true with how he sensed the importance of computers in service industries. Now, it's true in business education in the real world of the millions of small-business people in our country. In this, too, Jim Moran is at the cutting edge. What he has given us in the Jim Moran Institute for Global Entrepreneurship is a network, a system and a challenge.

I said it in the Jacksonville papers, "Thanks to Jim Moran there is no better place to study entrepreneurship and small business management, whether as a student or as a current business owner, than here at FSU."[5]

Maybe you think I'm bound to like Jim Moran for what he's doing for our school...or how I feel about him because he's been thoughtful to me and my wife on a personal level. My regard—I truly know—goes beyond that. Most of all, I esteem and admire Jim Moran because he epitomizes what I call the *caring leader*. His whole manner radiates, "Don't make a fuss over me."

When I first met Jim Moran, I came away with the impression, this guy can't be real. (I got to be a pretty good judge of what was real and what wasn't as a captain in Army Counterintelligence in the jungles of wartime Vietnam.) After all, how can someone this successful and determined truly place people first. Not only does Jim reconcile being a caring, generous, and courteous person with being an astute and extraordinarily successful entrepreneur, he knows how to turn genuine care into the best of human assets. That's something that the finest entrepreneurs understand best of all. They must rely on trust above all else. Jim was and still is "one of the guys from the neighborhood" for all his wisdom and perceptiveness, and people react to him with that same sense of ease and confidence.

I've had my share of chances to observe Jim Moran as he conducts business. We've been fortunate to assist Southeast Toyota in their own re-engineering efforts as they continue to remain state-of-the-art in their administrative structure. Their revamping was considerably less painful than in the vast majority of organizations. I suspect the reason why is the personal style that Jim coaches his team on. He's always stopping and talking with people. He radiates such a genuine spirit of trustworthiness, while managers in many other companies mistakenly believe that only the "hard skills" of management matter and that human concern is a sign of weakness.

A word more about business sense and being hard-nosed. No doubt about it, Jim's a skillful negotiator, and he has a sound sense of communicating and knowing the objectives that are important to his firm, but he is always keenly focused on the long-haul and the importance of human relationships. As an academic, my specialty is analyzing the impact of value systems on how consumers behave. So I have studied Jim's approach to marketing decisions very carefully.

I recall one time when Jim's people were negotiating the last stages of a deal that would sell a huge fleet of cars to a major rental car company. In the intensity of bringing a major negotiation to closure, Jim's people had a natural interest in holding out for the best price. Jim advised his people to stop negotiating for a better advantage, but he put his message across in the understated way only a wise teacher would. "These are friends of ours," he pointed out, "Over time, they've been very good to us." When his people thought about it, they concluded he was right, and the business relationship going forward has prospered as a result of Jim's perceptiveness. This is not only the mettle of a courteous man, but the characteristic of a person with great vision and foresight.

Part of Jim's great uniqueness stems from Jim having such a keen and current feel for the heartbeat of the business. His thinking about business matters is always fresh. Recently, industry bible *Automotive News* featured Jim Moran and proclaimed, "This is no absentee landlord."[t] He'll be close to the business for as long as the Lord permits because the world's Jim Morans—and they are few— don't retire. While Jim is not the retiring kind, he is also a realist...and realists know that it is important to leave a legacy. Just how do you go about leaving a legacy?

The generosity of the Morans is enormous, and it extends well beyond Florida State. In the past twelve months, they have given:

- Six hundred thousand dollars to Women in Distress to help violence-battered families in Broward County, Florida to open the Jim and Jan Moran Family Center.
- A $1,000,000 challenge grant by Jim and Jan Moran to the United Way of Broward County is designed to increase contributions from leadership givers. Its innovative structure utilizes the Broward Community Foundation to create an endowment and forges a unique partnership between the United Way of Broward County and the Broward Community Foundation, preparing the way for a better future in this region.
- Two million dollars to the Jacksonville Symphony Orchestra, helping—among other things—to give that orchestra a proper home and to bring fine music to all youngsters in grades 4 through 6 on Florida's First Coast, through the Young People's Concert Series. They'll learn about instruments, the beauty of music, and the importance of harmony music teaches us all, and they will learn about it free, from now until the end of time because of Jim, Jan, and JM Family.

- In partnership with the Super Bowl Host Committee Foundation and other Florida firms and organizations; the Jim Moran multi-million-dollar Challenge Grant provides $500,000 in challenge seed money to build three year-round recreational facilities for disadvantaged youth in Dade County. Run under the auspices of the Boys and Girls Clubs and the United Way, the first of these facilities will be built in Gwen Cherry Park in the heart of the Liberty City section of Miami. The second is the Moore Park Project, and the third is as yet unnamed. These NFL Youth Education Centers are desperately needed and will serve youngsters of all ages—from very young children to youths in their late teens—and should have special significance for both African-American and Hispanic youth in the community.
- Jim is no stranger to either the arts or to the dreams of young people, since he is both a Trustee of the Fort Lauderdale Art Museum and a member of the Board of Advisors for South Florida's Make-A-Wish Foundation.

Funding is certainly one of the aspects of the Morans' generosity. Of equal importance is the substantial time and personal involvement they give to projects. Marti and Wayne Huizenga recently asked Jim and Jan Moran to be chairpersons of a $15,000,000 capital and endowment campaign for the Boys and Girls Clubs of Broward County, the largest such campaign in the history of the Boys and Girls Clubs across the nation. There's a real shortage of recreational facilities for underprivileged youth in Broward County, and the Morans are particularly committed to linking the recreational program with education. Right now, Jim and Jan are spearheading a comprehensive fund-raising plan and are embarking on an ambitious meeting and personal speaking program to support it.

The world is waking up to Jim Moran and the many contributions he has made. In the past several months,

Nova Southeastern University inducted Jim into its Entrepreneur Hall of Fame, because he exemplifies the spirit and ideals of entrepreneurship.

Florida Atlantic University installed Jim into its Hall of Fame because of his remarkable business success.

The Institute of Human Relations of the American Jewish Committee presented Jim its Corporate Leadership Award.

The International Swimming Hall of Fame bestowed its Gold Medallion Award upon Jim because his life has served as an inspiration for youth and for significant achievement in business. Other honorees have included Johnny Weissmuller and Ronald Reagan.

The Crohn's and Colitis Foundation named Jim its Man of the Year for his role in building public awareness and in fundraising for this cause, as well as other charitable activities in the community.

The most exciting and distinguished accolade has been the decision to bestow on Jim the 1996 Horatio Alger Award. In the words of the governing Association: "The Horatio Alger Award was established in 1947 to encourage the young people of America to recognize that success can be achieved through hard work and perseverance." All of the Award's recipients have overcome adversity. They have "'pulled themselves up by their bootstraps' in the American tradition and achieved outstanding success." Public Broadcasting televises the awards live, and past recipients comprise a most distinguished list including: President Ronald Reagan, General Colin Powell, Dr. Norman Vincent Peale, Mary Kay Ash, Hank Aaron, Carol Burnett, and Sam Walton.

I am glad that this recognition is taking place, but it is not enough. As I see it, the world has been a lot more modest in giving back the recognition that it owes Jim Moran than Jim Moran has been in sharing with the world the rewards of his good fortune and hard work.

Material generosity is only part of Jim Moran's legacy, but the legacy that matters to me—to any of us—is the personal one, and Jim Moran has left two profound ones for me.

The first of these happened about five months after I became Business School dean. For the first time in my career, I was truly an administrator with a significant mission in the academic world. The scope of the Florida State business program is pretty large with a hundred faculty members, about three-hundred graduate students, and two-thousand undergraduates. Jim Moran knew that this was not an easy step for me. He helped me rise above the typical controversy that characterizes any distinguished academic faculty and to set a personal style I like to think has been much influenced by Jim Moran's own. In effect, he confirmed my sense of leadership, but he did it in such an understated way one would have hardly known that was his goal. I shall be long grateful for his tutorial because he taught me to find those contributions and skills within people that would really make a difference to our future and to the success and goals of our institution.

In a much acclaimed book on leadership called *Leadership Jazz*, Max De Pree, the now retired Chairman of another company with roots as a family enterprise—Herman Miller, Inc.—writes, "In the life of an American Indian tribe, the watercarrier held one of the most important and respected positions."[u] "Leaders," De Pree also says, "know who gives an organization health, who waters the roots of renewal."[v] Is it accidental, I have thought to myself since I read those words a couple of years ago, that Jim Moran cites so often the Japanese proverb saying, "The people who dig the well are entitled to drink the water"? The finest of leaders—caring and teaching leaders—understand and instruct all of us in the back-breaking and often thankless contributions that have to take place to make any complex organization work smoothly.

The other great personal legacy Jim Moran has given me was a conversation he had with my son William when he was about thirteen. We were attending YATC's annual golf tournament. During the reception and with a candor out of the blue that only a thirteen-year-old can muster, William turned to Jim Moran and asked, "How did you get all of this?" Jim took the question in stride. He could have shrugged off a youngster's inquiry with a quick answer. But, from his eyes, you could tell that he thought about the question very carefully for a minute or two. Then Jim stepped aside from the bustle of people around him and spent about fifteen minutes with William patiently explaining the most important basics about discipline, hard work, staying alert to changes in the world around you, and—most of all—the value of truly caring about people.

"It all started with a gas station..." Jim Moran began his conversation with William. My son has never forgotten that message. Nor have I. How many little "gas stations"...how many little dreams and ambitions can our young people grow into extraordinary triumphs with the proper encouragement and training? How many to-be-great men and women have little dreams nurtured into realities that extend beyond their wildest imagination because a caring someone will provide the means and the moments to make those dreams possible? That's Jim Moran's legacy...and, it's really the heart of all of our futures. "Before honor is humility," declares the Proverbs of the Old Testament. The courtesy, the wisdom and the humility of my friend Jim is living and modern proof of that insight...and cause enough for me to join in honoring Jim Moran.

Notes

a. Jon Winokur, *True Confessions* (New York: Dutton, 1992), p. 135.

b. Thomas Hoving, *Making the Mummies Dance* (New York: Simon & Schuster, 1993), p. 55.

c. Peter F. Drucker, *Managing for the Future* (New York: Truman Talley Books, 1992), p. 310.

d. Jerry Flint and Vicki Contavespi, "Wrong villain," *Forbes*, September 19, 1988.

e. "A Management Style Passes From Corporate Scene With the Death of Henry Ford II — Last of the Scions," *The Wall Street Journal*, September 30, 1987.

f. Christopher Power, Kathleen Kerwin, Ronald Grover, Keith Alexander and Robert D. Hof, "FLOPS," *Business Week*, August 16, 1993, pp. 34-39.

g. Jerry Flint and Vicki Contavespi, "Wrong villain," *Forbes*, September 19, 1988.

h. Jerry Crimmins, "Iroquois Theater Fire of 1903 is Still the Worst of Chicago's Deadly Blazes," *Chicago Tribune*, March 17, 1993.

i. Paul Molloy, "A Pleasure To Watch A Guy At Work," *Chicago Sun-Times*, May 28, 1962, Section 2, p 8.

j. "Heyday of the Haggle: The Buyer's Market In Cars," *TIME*, March 24, 1961.

k. Jon Winokur, *Friendly Advice* (New York: Dutton, 1990), p. 47.

l. Eiji Toyoda, *Toyota: Fifty Years in Motion* (New York: Harper & Row, 1987), p. 135.

m. Jon Winokur, *Friendly Advice* (New York: Dutton, 1990), p. 237.

n. George Stalk, Jr., and Alan M. Webber, "Japan's Dark Side of Time," *Harvard Business Review*, July-August 1993, pp. 93-102.

o. Quentin Hardy, "Duffers in Japan Turn Round of Golf Into the Killing Game," *The Wall Street Journal Europe*, June 22, 1993.

p. Lester Thurow, *Head to Head* (New York: William Morrow and Company, Inc., 1992), p. 139.

q. Deborah Work, "Here's a car dealer blacks can believe," *Fort Lauderdale Sun Sentinel*, March 20, 1995.

r. Elizabeth Lesly, "Bright Stars and Burnouts," *Business Week*, May 22, 1995, p. 70.

s. "Moran establishes entrepreneurship center at FSU," *Financial News & Daily Record*, May 30, 1995, Vol. 83, No. 107.

t. Lindsay Chappell, "Sunny Days For Moran," *Automotive News*, January 23, 1995, page 3.

u. Max DePree, *Leadership Jazz* (New York: Dell Publishing, 1992), p. 65.

v. Max DePree, *Leadership Jazz* (New York: Dell Publishing, 1992), p. 143.

Index